Flex your SPaG muscles with Weekly Workouts!

Key Stage 3 Spelling, Punctuation & Grammar is all about practice. That's why CGP has made this brilliant book to sharpen your SPaG skills throughout Year 8.

Every workout has a mix of spelling, punctuation and grammar questions to check you really know your stuff. Plus, there's one for each week of the school year so you'll get stacks of practice.

All the answers are at the back, as well as a score sheet so you can track your progress. CGP — we've got everything you need for S, P and G!

How to Use this Book

- This book contains <u>36 workouts</u>. We've split them into <u>3 sections</u> — one for each term — with <u>12 workouts</u> each. There's roughly one workout for <u>every week</u> of the school year.

- Each workout is out of <u>12 marks</u> and should take about <u>10 minutes</u> to complete.

- The workouts start with two short <u>warm-up questions</u>, followed by a mixture of <u>spelling, punctuation and grammar</u> questions.

- They <u>progress in difficulty</u>, so they're perfect for ensuring that pupils are <u>getting to grips</u> with the spelling, punctuation and grammar skills they need for Year 8 English.

- The <u>tick boxes</u> on the contents page can help to keep a <u>record</u> of which workouts have been attempted.

- <u>Answers</u> and a <u>score sheet</u> can be found at the <u>back</u> of the book.

Published by CGP
ISBN: 978 1 83774 056 7

Editors: Siân Butler, Andy Cashmore, Heather Cowley, Emma Duffee, Catherine Heygate, Ilana Pearce, Hayley Shaw, Kirsty Sweetman

With thanks to Hannah Roscoe and John Sanders for the proofreading.

With thanks to Jade Sim for the copyright research.

Clipart from Corel®

Printed by Elanders Ltd, Newcastle upon Tyne.
Based on the classic CGP style created by Richard Parsons.

Text, design, layout and original illustrations
© Coordination Group Publications Ltd. (CGP) 2023
All rights reserved.

Photocopying this book is not permitted, even if you have a CLA licence.
Extra copies are available from CGP with next day delivery • 0800 1712 712 • www.cgpbooks.co.uk

Contents

Autumn Term

- [ ] **Workout 1** 2
- [ ] **Workout 2** 4
- [ ] **Workout 3** 6
- [ ] **Workout 4** 8
- [ ] **Workout 5** 10
- [ ] **Workout 6** 12
- [ ] **Workout 7** 14
- [ ] **Workout 8** 16
- [ ] **Workout 9** 18
- [ ] **Workout 10** 20
- [ ] **Workout 11** 22
- [ ] **Workout 12** 24

Spring Term

- [ ] **Workout 1** 26
- [ ] **Workout 2** 28
- [ ] **Workout 3** 30
- [ ] **Workout 4** 32
- [ ] **Workout 5** 34
- [ ] **Workout 6** 36
- [ ] **Workout 7** 38
- [ ] **Workout 8** 40
- [ ] **Workout 9** 42
- [ ] **Workout 10** 44
- [ ] **Workout 11** 46
- [ ] **Workout 12** 48

Summer Term

- [ ] **Workout 1** 50
- [ ] **Workout 2** 52
- [ ] **Workout 3** 54
- [ ] **Workout 4** 56
- [ ] **Workout 5** 58
- [ ] **Workout 6** 60
- [ ] **Workout 7** 62
- [ ] **Workout 8** 64
- [ ] **Workout 9** 66
- [ ] **Workout 10** 68
- [ ] **Workout 11** 70
- [ ] **Workout 12** 72

Answers 74

Score Sheet 86

Autumn Term: Workout 1

Warm up

1. Write down the plural forms of the underlined words on the lines below.

   a) I bought <u>potato</u> and <u>orange</u>.   ....

   b) The <u>kangaroo</u> go to <u>party</u>.   ....

   (1 mark)

2. Tick the three words that are adverbs.

   a) apply ☐   b) very ☐   c) bubbly ☐

   d) lazily ☐   e) ugly ☐   f) suddenly ☐

   (1 mark)

3. Add inverted commas and punctuation in the correct places in the sentence below.

   Hey I shouted Can you help me with these heavy bags?

   (1 mark)

4. Complete each sentence with a suitable word containing 'ough'.

   The thunder distracted Gabi and she lost her train of ....

   Jam .... are my favourite type of sweet treat.

   I think we should go .... that mysterious door.

   (1 mark)

5. Circle the correct word to complete each sentence below.

   You are the candidate **who / whom** impressed me the most.

   Please tell me to **who / whom** I should address this letter.

   Who / Whom turned the volume up so loud?

   (1 mark)

6. Rewrite the sentences below, using either a colon or a semicolon.

   Sunil forgot one thing the gym wasn't open.

   ....

   My dad wanted a pet bird I wanted a snake.

   ....
   (2 marks)

7. Choose the correct word in brackets to complete the following sentences.

   I am not .... sure that we're allowed in there. *(holy / wholly)*

   My grandparents are on a Mediterranean .... *(crews / cruise)*

   Let's not .... our afternoon sitting on the sofa. *(waist / waste)*

   I spent ages brushing the horse's .... mane. *(course / coarse)*
   (2 marks)

8. Rewrite the single sentence below as four shorter, clearer sentences. You may need to add or remove words.

   > Lulu glided adeptly across the water, her hands clutching the metal bar, making it instantly clear to any spectators that this was not her first time on the wakeboard, since she was, in fact, an expert.

   ....

   ....

   ....

   ....
   (3 marks)

Score: /12

Autumn Term: Workout 2

Warm up

1. Draw lines to match the start of each word to the correct word ending.

   substan   benefi   antiso   impar

   tial   cial

   (1 mark)

2. In each pair, underline the sentence that uses apostrophes correctly.

   a) That's Mrs Roberts's house.   The womens' football team plays on Tuesday's.

   b) We were'nt told about it.   The orchestra's rehearsal isn't going well.

   (1 mark)

3. Underline the conjunction in each sentence.

   Riva wants me to go to the concert with her, but I'm quite tired.

   He likes dressing up as a pirate because it makes him look tougher.

   We can go to the park down the road if it stops raining soon.

   (1 mark)

4. Add a comma in the correct place below, then explain why the comma is needed.

   Since I left my umbrella at home I should probably borrow yours.

   ....

   (2 marks)

5. For each sentence, decide what type of noun the words in bold are.
   Then, write 'concrete', 'abstract' or 'collective' on the line.

   It caused a big **delay** in my journey.   ....

   Look at that majestic **pride** of lions.   ....

   He put all of the shells on the **shelf**.   ....

   (1 mark)

6. Add a suffix to the words in brackets to complete the sentences below.

Happily, Freddie was .... (success) in herding the sheep.

We got into an .... (argue) over our favourite singer.

I am not .... (response) for that stain on the carpet.

He was blinded by the .... (bright) of the torchlight.

(2 marks)

7. Rewrite the sentence below, adding a hyphen to make its meaning clearer.

Hae bought delicious cakes from her favourite family owned bakery.

....

....

(1 mark)

8. Rewrite the passage below so all the verbs are in the present progressive form.

> You crave a bowl of my world-famous soup. We begin with a chopped onion, then tomatoes, garlic and stock. You taste the soup occasionally while it cooks. When the mixture bubbles, I squeeze in the secret ingredient — ketchup.

....

....

....

....

....

....

(3 marks)

Score: /12

Autumn Term: Workout 3

Warm up

1. In each pair, circle the word that is spelt correctly.
   a) confidance   confidence   b) distance   distence
   c) importance   importence   d) audiance   audience
   (1 mark)

2. In each pair, underline the sentence which uses commas correctly.
   a) In the distance, I saw a huge tree.   In the distance I saw a huge, tree.
   b) Sadly he stole my bow tie, last week.   Sadly, he stole my bow tie last week.
   (1 mark)

3. Choose the correct word ending from the boxes to complete each word.

   | cious | tious | cion | tion |

   ficti...............   mali...............   corrup...............
   (1 mark)

4. For each sentence, write down whether it needs brackets or a dash.

   I opened the wooden box and gasped it was empty.   ....

   Shelly my tortoise likes to ride his skateboard.   ....

   The first Olympics in 776 BC were held in Greece.   ....
   (1 mark)

5. Tick each sentence that uses the passive voice.

   Is this the way to the safari park? ☐   Our team's flag was captured. ☐

   Instructions have been provided. ☐   Rhiannon rushed out the door. ☐
   (1 mark)

6. Underline the adverbs in the sentence below. Then, rewrite the sentence with different adverbs to make it more certain.

   It's possibly not the best weather for an ice cream, but I'll likely have one.

   ....

   ....
   (2 marks)

7. Rewrite the words in italics with the correct comparatives or superlatives.

   Mahmoud's dog is *fast* than mine, but my dog is the *big*.

   ....

   She has *many* siblings than Esther, but Esther's are the *noisy*.

   ....
   (2 marks)

8. Six words in the passage below have been scrambled.
   Rewrite the passage, unscrambling the words so that they are spelt correctly.

   > At gheit last night, my next-door buornegih pranked me by hiding my favourite gnome. I couldn't beevile her cheek. When I treiveerd him, she skriheed with laughter and denied being the gnome feith.

   ....

   ....

   ....

   ....
   (3 marks)

Score: /12

Autumn Term: Workout 4

Warm up

1. In each pair, underline the sentence that uses negatives correctly.

    a) There's no chance we're not winning.   There's no chance we're losing.

    b) He doesn't have time for a nap.   He doesn't have no time for a nap.
    (1 mark)

2. Tick each word that is spelt correctly.

    a) moisture ☐   b) picsure ☐   c) exposure ☐

    d) clossure ☐   e) pleassure ☐   f) creature ☐
    (1 mark)

3. For each sentence, write 'P' if the apostrophe is used to show possession, or 'C' if it's used to show contraction.

    Don't tell her about my mind-reading powers. ....

    This camel's humps are the tallest of them all. ....

    They're going to watch a cricket match today. ....
    (1 mark)

4. Finish the sentence by adding a suitable second clause.

    We had two options: ....

    ....
    (1 mark)

5. Complete the sentences using a conjunction which has a similar meaning to the one given in brackets. Use a different conjunction each time.

    I would like that maroon jumper .... it's expensive. (*even if*)

    Kyla likes to go fishing .... I find it a bit dull. (*while*)
    (2 marks)

6. Rewrite the list, adding bullet points and the correct punctuation after each point.

   My mum's shopping list included these items: pineapple juice, one pint of skimmed milk, six sausages and a bag of self-raising flour (the supermarket brand).

   ....
   ....
   ....
   ....
   ....
   (2 marks)

7. Write down the prepositions from the box that tell you when things happen.

   | during | above | until | after | onto | among | before |

   ....
   (1 mark)

8. Rewrite the passage so that all the verbs agree with their subjects.

   My friend have bought a lie detector machine and we is going to take turns doing a test. It'll be fun but I is a bit nervous. He is going to ask questions and if the machine beep, it means my answers is lies. I hopes I pass the test!

   ....
   ....
   ....
   ....
   ....
   (3 marks)

   Score: ☐ /12

Autumn Term: Workout 5

> **Warm up**
>
> 1. In each pair, underline the sentence that includes an adjective.
>
>   a) My sleeveless shirt is in the wash.   That shirt has no sleeves.
>
>   b) We need to turn left.   I've lost my left glove.
>
>   *(1 mark)*
>
> 2. Tick each sentence which contains a soft 'c'.
>
>   Claudia couldn't stand the taste of citrus fruits. ☐
>
>   The architect's quick sketch won the contest. ☐
>
>   The council has recently decided to expand the school. ☐
>
>   *(1 mark)*

3. Rewrite each verb in the tense given in brackets.

   It *froze*.   .... (*simple present*)

   I *catch*.   .... (*simple past*)

   (1 mark)

4. Add a comma in the correct place below, then explain why the comma is needed.

   Unless the weather improves the match will be called off.

   ....

   (2 marks)

5. Underline the longest noun phrase in each of the sentences below.

   A solitary boat floated on the unusually calm, crystal water.

   The horse's long, flowing mane was plaited for the showjumping contest.

   The ominous, grey thunder clouds covered the once-peaceful valley.

   (1 mark)

6. Write which nouns the pronouns in italics are replacing.

   My drums annoy my mum, but I think *they* sound great. ....

   Fahad and I went to see Penny, but *we* didn't stay long. ....

   My friend didn't want her bike, so she gave *it* to me. ....

   Polly plays tennis with her dad, and *she* plays rugby. ....

   (2 marks)

7. There are three spelling errors in the sentence below. Rewrite the sentence correctly on the lines.

   The bird flew gracfully over the field, preparing to snatch its pray with claws as sharp as knifes.

   ....

   ....
   (1 mark)

8. Rewrite the passage below, replacing each underlined word with a synonym.

   > Rudy <u>threw</u> open the curtains and <u>smiled</u>. Fresh, <u>sparkling</u> snow blanketed everything. He was <u>thrilled</u> — school would be cancelled, so he would <u>escape</u> an entire day of lessons. He called his neighbour, Amelie, and <u>asked</u> if she wanted to go sledging.

   ....

   ....

   ....

   ....

   ....
   (3 marks)

   Score: ☐ /12

Autumn Term: Workout 6

Warm up

1. Add 'a', 'an' or 'the' to the sentences below.

   Dani gave surfing .... try but she was scared of .... waves.

   Alexis had .... excellent run and was .... fastest skier.

   (1 mark)

2. Circle the conjunction in each sentence.

   He wanted to visit her but she lived too far away.

   If I had wings, I would fly to Spain.

   (1 mark)

3. In each group, underline the two words that contain the same 'ough' sound.

   a) trough   borough   cough   although

   b) enough   brought   sought   dough

   (1 mark)

4. Use a line (|) to separate the main clause and the subordinate clause in each sentence below.

   When the project is complete, we will throw an enormous party.

   They are the people who decided to live in the depths of the forest.

   We are staying in the entrance of the building until Harry arrives.

   The winning team beamed with pride when the final whistle blew.

   (2 marks)

5. Complete the sentences below by adding the suffix '-able' or '-ible' to each root word in brackets.

   The tower is .... (*note*) for its .... (*consider*) height.

   The top floor is only .... (*access*) via a steep stairway.

   (1 mark)

6. Some of the words in the passage below have the wrong prefixes. Underline the mistakes, then rewrite the words with more suitable prefixes on the lines.

> The autonational technology convention exhibited inventions from all over the world. They included a backwards clock: its hands move interclockwise. There was also an automatic birthday cake machine with an autoactive screen to choose the icing. It made incredible antisized cakes. Unfortunately, I was not impressed by the interclimactic flying carpet display — it couldn't get off the ground. Needless to say, nobody asked the dismayed inventor for an antigraph.

....

....

....

(3 marks)

7. Rewrite the sentences below, removing unneeded words, using either a colon or semicolon.

   The dish needs these things. It needs mushrooms, peppers and onions.

   ....

   Pablo has four dogs and Jamie has a rabbit and three cats.

   ....

   (2 marks)

8. Complete the table below.

Formal style	Informal style
	Gimme the key now.
I shall endeavour to attend.	
	I bet it's brill.

(1 mark)

Score: /12

Autumn Term: Workout 7

Warm up

1. Draw lines to match each sentence to the correct label.

   Which of those plates of food is mine?   statement

   Katy swore she would never eat spinach again.   question

   How amazing that performance was!   command

   Come into the kitchen immediately!   exclamation

   (1 mark)

2. In each pair, underline the passive sentence.

   a) Granny prepared a picnic.   The picnic was prepared by Granny.

   b) Faisal was embraced by Immy.   Immy embraced Faisal.

   (1 mark)

3. Rewrite the sentence below using the correct punctuation.

   my favourite music genres are pop country and reggae

   ....

   (1 mark)

4. Underline the modal verb in each sentence.

   Valeria would have gone to the party but she was already busy.

   Tomek is going to arrive at 7 so I must prepare dinner before then.

   Asa has been saving his pocket money so he can buy a saxophone.

   (1 mark)

5. Add a suffix to these words to turn them into adjectives.

   disaster ....   flaw ....

   religion ....   speech ....

   (2 marks)

6. Rewrite the sentences below using pronouns to avoid repetition.

Samara bought herself a new bike and Samara rode the new bike home.

....

My friends enjoy eating pizza so my friends eat pizza every Friday.

....

(2 marks)

7. Tick each group of words that is a clause.

the charity shops in town ☐   as I was scrapbooking ☐

he makes his own cheese ☐   on their new food blog ☐

(1 mark)

8. Add three paragraph markers (//) to the passage below.
Then, write down the reason why you started each paragraph.

> The boat swayed fiercely from side to side. Suddenly, there was an almighty crash and Callie plunged into the dark water. She began to swim. After what seemed like a lifetime, she made it to the shore and collapsed in a heap, panting heavily. "Hello! Is anyone here?" she shouted. "Where am I?" In the nearby village, Nauris had decided to stroll to the beach. He was enjoying the fresh air when he heard what sounded like someone shouting for help. He hurried towards the sound.

second paragraph: ....

third paragraph: ....

fourth paragraph: ....

(3 marks)

Score: ☐ / 12

Autumn Term: Workout 8

Warm up

1. In each pair, underline the sentence where the verb agrees with its subject.

   a) They always like baking.   We likes to cook together.

   b) My sister Niamh eat a lot.   He usually eats out on Fridays.

   (1 mark)

2. In each sentence, circle the verb that is in a different tense to the others.

   Yesterday, Ben played golf, I went shopping and Rex sleeps.

   She believes that sandwiches were the best food and eats them daily.

   (1 mark)

3. Add a colon in the correct place in each sentence below.

   Olga loves to dance she dances for three hours a week.

   Felix's goldfish has an unusal name it is called Pumpkin.

   (1 mark)

4. Sort the words below into the correct columns.

   bottle   flock   loyalty   trust   fleet   taxi

Concrete noun	Collective noun	Abstract noun

   (2 marks)

5. Underline the word or words in each sentence that should be hyphenated.

   Omid cooked a roast dinner for his brother and sister in law.

   Mina recounted the money to check that she had enough.

   Hallie set a short term goal of exercising every day for a week.

   (1 mark)

6. Add the suffixes '-ed' and '-ing' to each root word.

   identify .... (+ed)   .... (+ing)

   rebel .... (+ed)   .... (+ing)

   (1 mark)

7. Add brackets or a dash to each sentence below.
   Claude Monet a famous artist painted water lilies.
   We couldn't believe our eyes the dolphin was waving at us.
   Shrove Tuesday known as Pancake Day is the day before Lent begins.
   Matilda laughed sheepishly nobody else was in fancy dress.

   (2 marks)

8. There are six spelling mistakes in the passage below.
   Rewrite the passage, correcting all of the mistakes.

   > Winning seemed imconceivable. The referee's injust decision to disallow a goal jeopardised the Pudgley Pioneers' chances. But after the coach's electrifiing pep talk, they equalised. Then, in highly inregular circumstances, the keeper's goal kick found their opponents' net, secureing the Pioneers' victory.

   ....

   ....

   ....

   ....

   ....

   ....

   (3 marks)

   Score: /12

Autumn Term: Workout 9

> **Warm up**
>
> 1. Draw lines to match each word to the correct box.
>
>   friendly
>
>   quickly   adjective
>
>   homely
>   adverb
>   suddenly
>
>   *(1 mark)*
>
> 2. In each pair, underline the sentence that has no spelling mistakes.
>
>   a) We are studying the plage in history.   The actor delivered her monologue.
>
>   b) The scenery is extremely picturesque.   I try to improve my singing technikes.
>
>   *(1 mark)*

3. Underline the correct determiner in the sentences below.

   My robot is asking if **a / an / the** humans can give him **a / an / the** hug.

   I had **a / an / the** interest in **a / an / the** most popular poet of the century.

   (1 mark)

4. Write down the subject of each sentence on the lines.

   Later, the sun melted the snowman.   ....

   On Friday, I will go kayaking with Wren.   ....

   This drawer is full of different socks.   ....

   (1 mark)

5. Fill in the gaps with the correct word ending to complete the sentences below.

   I was reluct...................... to enter the unexplored cave.

   The scientists conducted an experim...................... in the lab.

   (1 mark)

6. Add a comma in the correct place in the sentence below.
   Then, explain why the comma is needed.

   On the top floor of the manor there was a dimly lit attic.

   ....

   (2 marks)

7. Each sentence below contains a spelling mistake.
   Rewrite the sentences correctly on the lines.

   He's a new edition to our league.

   ....

   Except this gift as a token of my gratitude.

   ....

   (2 marks)

8. There are six punctuation mistakes in the passage below.
   Rewrite the passage, correcting all of the mistakes.

   > Though they all warned me against living in an igloo my friends remarks' didn't deter me. So here's what I did; I packed a bag travelled across the globe (on several planes) and arrived in Greenlands' capital, Nuuk, all alone.

   ....

   ....

   ....

   ....

   ....

   ....

   (3 marks)

   Score: /12

Autumn Term: Workout 10

Warm up

1. Circle the verbs in the sentences below.

   While I jogged, my hair swished in the breeze.

   She implied that the chorus of the song is boring.

   (1 mark)

2. In each pair, underline the sentence that uses contractions correctly.

   a) I hope he let's me sit at the front.   Callum hadn't seen his dog in hours.

   b) The mysterious box would'nt open.   There wasn't any milk in the fridge.

   (1 mark)

3. Choose the correct prefix from the boxes to complete each word.

   | de | dis | mis |

   …………rail   …………infect   …………hear   …………advantage

   (1 mark)

4. Underline the possessive pronoun in each of the sentences below.

   My pet hamster is definitely greedier than yours.

   I lent her mine because her tambourine had broken.

   Jacob might want a treehouse if we show him ours.

   (1 mark)

5. Add an adverbial phrase to the sentence below.

   I decided to take the bus.

   ………………………………………………………………………………………………

   (1 mark)

6. Complete the table below by correctly adding each suffix to the root words.

Root word	-ed	-ing
empty		
achieve		
patrol		

(2 marks)

7. Tick the sentence that is missing some punctuation.
   Then, rewrite the sentence with the correct punctuation.

   Anya asked me to help her with her art project. ☐

   Could you please tell me the time asked Aliz. ☐

   ....

   (2 marks)

8. There are six incorrect verbs in the passage below.
   Rewrite the passage, correcting all the verbs.

   > Tomorrow, I am go to a water park, and I are planning to spend all day in the water. I couldn't wait: last time I went I flyed down the slides and floats along the lazy river. I just hoped it doesn't rain tomorrow!

   ....

   ....

   ....

   ....

   ....

   (3 marks)

   Score: ☐ /12

Autumn Term: Workout 11

Warm up

1. In each pair, circle the word where the unstressed vowel sound is underlined.

    a) W<u>e</u>dnesday   Wedn<u>e</u>sday   b) c<u>o</u>mpany   comp<u>a</u>ny

    c) vol<u>u</u>ntary   volunt<u>a</u>ry   d) anim<u>a</u>l   an<u>i</u>mal

    (1 mark)

2. Underline the subordinate clause in each sentence.

    In case it was dark outside, Alexa brought a torch.

    We'll have to hurry up in order to reach the top in time for sunset.

    (1 mark)

3. Add a prefix to the words below to complete the sentences.

    They moved me from the beginner class to the ....mediate class.

    The ....motive museum is where they keep all the old cars.

    Clean your hands with ....bacterial soap for thirty seconds.

    (1 mark)

4. Underline the modal verb in each sentence.

    That possum is prone to biting, however friendly he may seem.

    Shall we have a slice of chocolate cake with our cup of tea?

    (1 mark)

5. Tick each sentence which uses a semicolon correctly.

    Kellie climbed straight over the fence; Tina tried to open the lock. ☐

    We ordered; two burgers, a milkshake, a salad and some chips. ☐

    The songbirds chirped; the dragonflies flitted through the rushes. ☐

    (1 mark)

6. Underline the two informal words in each sentence below.
Then, write down a more formal word that could replace each informal word.

This mouldy cheese is well gross. ....

That bloke just told a rubbish story! ....

(2 marks)

7. Rewrite the sentences below in the present progressive form.

I take my cousin to the dentist.

....

We drove for six hours to get to the beach.

....

(2 marks)

8. There are six verbs that are not in the correct form in the passage below.
Rewrite the passage, correcting all the verbs.

> On our adventureous trip to the fameous Great Barrier Reef, we learnt that corrotion is a threat to the area. The damage humans have done may not be reversable — we must take caucian and try to be more sustainible in future.

....

....

....

....

....

(3 marks)

Score: /12

Autumn Term: Workout 12

Warm up

1. Underline the words that have a soft 'c' in the sentence below.

    I exercise by going to a dance class once a week and riding my bike.

    (1 mark)

2. Tick each sentence that uses commas correctly.

    Once he has eaten his lunch, Adam will go for a walk. ☐

    Even though we lost the match, our spirits remained high. ☐

    Nabila felt much more relaxed, after her trip to the spa. ☐

    (1 mark)

3. Draw lines to show whether each conjunction expresses time, place or cause.

    Our map was upside down <u>so</u> we went the wrong way.

    The mini sandwiches were gone <u>after</u> the squirrels stole them.

    She wears her favourite scrunchie <u>everywhere</u> she goes.

    Could you take off your shoes <u>before</u> you enter our home?

    | time |
    | place |
    | cause |

    (1 mark)

4. Underline the longest noun phrase in each sentence below.

    Unfortunately, I think your new cat-themed calendar is missing a page.

    There is a fluffy sheep jumping on a huge, blue and red bouncy castle.

    I think the mysterious hole at the end of the garden leads to a secret cave.

    (1 mark)

5. For each of the words below, write down the root word and the suffix.

    steadily   root word: .... + suffix: ....

    maturity   root word: .... + suffix: ....

    (1 mark)

6. Write the meaning of each sentence on the line.

We replaced the lamp on the shelf.

....

We re-placed the lamp on the shelf.

....
(2 marks)

7. Underline the adverb in each sentence. Then, write whether each adverb makes the sentence certain (C) or uncertain (U).

We are potentially in the wrong place as this is not a zoo. ....

Rory is organised, so he inevitably arrives before the start. ....

You should definitely wear a special suit as a beekeeper. ....

Even though I find blue cheese smelly, perhaps I will try it. ....
(2 marks)

8. Rewrite the passage below so that all the verbs are in the past progressive form.

> *The air becomes colder. I approach the door steadily. Sweat begins to form on my brow and goosebumps pop up on my arms. The floorboards groan at full volume. Under pressure, I start to panic.*

....

....

....

....

....
(3 marks)

Score: /12

Spring Term: Workout 1

Warm up

1. In each pair, circle the word that is spelt correctly.

   a) backlog   backlogue   b) physique   physiqe

   c) anoraque   anorak   d) dialog   dialogue

   (1 mark)

2. Underline all the prepositions in the sentences below.

   The dog jumped off the sofa and ran under the table.

   Within days, the caterpillar had turned into a butterfly.

   (1 mark)

3. Rewrite each verb in the form given in brackets.

   Lia *learns* to read palms.   .... *(past perfect)*

   We *eat* lots of pasta.   .... *(present perfect)*

   (1 mark)

4. Add commas to the passage below so that it is punctuated correctly.

   Lucas known to his friends as Luke loves films. Paige Luke's sister works for a film studio. Last Friday Paige's boss gave her some tickets to a premiere. Being a kind sister Paige decided to take Luke to the premiere with her.

   (2 marks)

5. Complete each sentence with a different modal verb. The words in brackets tell you whether each sentence should be certain or possible.

   They .... have taken a shortcut to get home before us. *(certain)*

   Jordan's friends .... have arrived at the station by now. *(certain)*

   We .... have gone to the wrong café by accident. *(possible)*

   (1 mark)

6. Write the determiner in each sentence on the lines.

   They are riding those horses today.   ....

   There are not many scones left.   ....

   We run our business together.   ....

   (1 mark)

7. Rewrite the passage below as a single sentence using semicolons.

   <u>I spoke to these people</u>:
   - Jess, the lawyer — she lives next door
   - Masood, Barry's friend
   - Kev, the security guard

   ....

   ....

   (2 marks)

8. There are six spelling mistakes in the passage below.
   Rewrite the passage, correcting the mistakes.

   > Minnie had to be sutle to avoid her enemies. She had disgised herself in armur and now approached the casle. Huge dogs guarded the gates, nawing on bones. Minnie clenched her fists so tightly her nuckles turned white.

   ....

   ....

   ....

   ....

   ....

   (3 marks)

   Score: /12

Spring Term: Workout 2

> **Warm up**
>
> 1. In each group of words, circle the word that is not part of the same word family as the other words.
>
>   a) dearly   dearest   endearing   endeavour
>
>   b) restful   arrest   unrest   restlessness
>
>   *(1 mark)*
>
> 2. Tick the sentence that uses pronouns correctly.
>
>   Scott invited us to the cinema for his birthday and us saw a great film. ☐
>
>   Tori told Danielle she fancied a walk, so the two of them went out. ☐
>
>   *(1 mark)*

3. Add the suffix to each root word and write the new word on the line.

   infer + ing   ....

   offer + ed   ....

   refer + al   ....

   (1 mark)

4. Draw lines to match each underlined clause to the correct box.

   Fenhua passed the old bench <u>where he used to sit</u>.

   <u>Milo is going to the gig instead</u> as Faye can't go.

   Djamila, <u>who I sit with in history</u>, is a hockey player.

   <u>I went to a music festival</u> which lasted all week.

        [main clause]

        [relative clause]

   (1 mark)

5. Complete each sentence below using an adverb.

   The group is going to the skate park ....

   I am meeting my stepbrother .... for an ice lolly.

   (1 mark)

6. Add the correct punctuation to the passage below.

   "Is that what I think it is?" whispered Imamu.
   Ayaan screamed, " What an utterly horrifying creature "
   Let's get out of here before it wakes up " uttered Paisley.

   (2 marks)

7. Underline the sentence in each pair that isn't written in Standard English. Then, rewrite these sentences using Standard English on the lines below.

   a) I found Sakura to be very friendly.   Joel and me get on really good.

   ....

   b) I think them dance so elegant.   I am very fond of dancing.

   ....

   (2 marks)

8. There are six spelling mistakes in the passage below.
   Rewrite the passage, correcting all of the mistakes.

   Writing a book takes patience and resiliance, so ultimatly you should choose a subject that's of significence to you. Franklly, if you're hesitant about the topic, you'll be likly to abandon your book in an instent.

   ....

   ....

   ....

   ....

   ....

   ....

   (3 marks)

   Score: ☐ / 12

Spring Term: Workout 3

Warm up

1. In each pair, underline the word that uses the 'un-' prefix correctly.

   a) unhumane   unthinkable   b) unknowingly   unhearten

   c) uninspiring   undependent   d) unarray   undecided

   (1 mark)

2. Circle the incorrect apostrophes in the sentences below.

   The student's new books' were going to be used in Mr Fosters' class.

   Chanels' favourite sport is rugby; she play's for her school's team.

   (1 mark)

3. Tick each sentence that uses the subjunctive.

   We must prove that we were out of town at the time. ☐

   I would ban loud chewing if I were Prime Minister. ☐

   It is absolutely essential that Omari get plenty of rest. ☐

   (1 mark)

4. Add a dash to each sentence to separate the main clauses.

   The bowling alley is closed let's come back tomorrow.

   I haven't skied in years last time I broke my ankle.

   Ron is out he is having lunch at a café in town.

   (1 mark)

5. Complete each sentence with a suitable subordinating conjunction.
   Use a different conjunction each time.

   Cami learnt to speak some Japanese .... she moved to Tokyo.

   I no longer eat dairy products .... I am now a vegan.

   Patrick won't read a book .... it is in the fantasy genre.

   (1 mark)

6. Complete the table below.

Adjective	Comparative	Superlative
	worse	
expensive		
		silliest

(2 marks)

7. Rewrite the sentences below in the tense given in brackets.

This autumn, we moved to Newcastle and bought a house. (*simple present*)

....

I have spoken to Benedika and we have chosen to leave the band. (*simple past*)

....

(2 marks)

8. There are six spelling mistakes in the passage below.
Rewrite the passage, correcting the mistakes.

> I was consious that I wanted to be more sotial in my community, so I took up a new hobby: marshal arts. In my inicial lessons, I was pretty atrosious. I was trying far too many overambicious moves for a beginner.

....

....

....

....

....

....

(3 marks)

Score: /12

Spring Term: Workout 4

Warm up

1. In each pair, circle the word that is spelt correctly.

    a) stableise   stabilise   b) personify   personnify

    c) truly   truely   d) drasticly   drastically

    (1 mark)

2. Use a line (|) to separate the clauses in each of the sentences below.

    It's supposed to rain so we have got an umbrella.

    Holly wants to be a landscaper and she is very talented.

    Josiah wants to attend university before he goes travelling.

    (1 mark)

3. Tick each sentence where the subject is underlined.

    The teammates are in <u>the gym</u>. ☐   Afterwards, <u>I</u> will go to training. ☐

    Did <u>Aia</u> pass on Sam's message? ☐   Orla is having lunch with <u>Malik</u>. ☐

    (1 mark)

4. Add colons and semicolons to the passage below so that it is punctuated correctly.

    Here's the agenda paint the kitchen ceiling where the roof leaked tear off the wallpaper under the stairs and replace the showerhead in the bathroom.

    (1 mark)

5. There are three spelling errors in the sentence below. Rewrite the sentence, correcting the mistakes.

    The manufacshured furnichure was remeassured to ensure it was correct.

    ....

    ....

    (1 mark)

6. Add two paragraph markers (//) to the passage below.
   Then, explain why you started each paragraph.

   Joe shone the torch over the dirt-covered plaque. "Vinegrove Mansion," he said, reading the sign aloud. Later that night, the house was all he could think about. He pondered why so grand an estate had been left abandoned.

   second paragraph: ....

   third paragraph: ....
   (2 marks)

7. Complete each sentence using the type of noun given in brackets.

   Kito is going rollerblading with Mercy on ....   *(proper noun)*

   The .... of mountains was majestic.   *(collective noun)*

   Flo accepted her award with ....   *(abstract noun)*

   Caden grabbed his .... and ran out the door.   *(concrete noun)*
   (2 marks)

8. Rewrite the passage so that all the verbs agree with their subjects.

   > Council members has approved plans to build a housing estate on our park. My son feel so upset — the children uses this space every day. My neighbours and I am furious, so we is planning to object when the members next meets.

   ....

   ....

   ....

   ....

   ....
   (3 marks)

   Score: ☐ /12

Spring Term: Workout 5

> **Warm up**
>
> 1. The sentence below is missing a pair of brackets.
>   Circle the pair of letters which shows where the brackets should be.
>
>   This Italian painter **D** of whom I can't say **E** I'm a fan **F** is very famous.
>
>   a) D & E   b) D & F   c) E & F
>
>   *(1 mark)*
>
> 2. In each pair, underline the sentence that includes a possessive pronoun.
>
>   a) My dad drove me there.   The house with the blue door is theirs.
>
>   b) My bag is similar to hers.   It is time we tidied up our garden.
>
>   *(1 mark)*

3. Add the correct silent letters to complete the words in the sentences below.

   I desi___ned some s___enery for the play's autumnal setting.

   Gloria thinks the dress is w___ite, but I'd say it's closer to a sa___mon pink.

   (1 mark)

4. Underline the modal verb in each sentence.

   Eitan thought he must have imagined the flying raccoon.

   Will you carry the shopping bags for the rest of the journey?

   If you want some company, I could join you on your trip.

   (1 mark)

5. Underline the mistake in each sentence. Write the correct word on the lines.

   You aught to go through to reception to check in.   ....

   Millie was distrought when her cough got worse.   ....

   Nobody laughed when I fell on the ruff concrete.   ....

   The research was tough but he had a breakthrew.   ....

   (2 marks)

6. Underline the word or words in each sentence that make it informal.

   This is Casey's telephone number, isn't it?

   Aren't you supposed to be at hockey practice?

   Let me know if you wanna come swimming with us.

   (1 mark)

7. Rewrite these sentences using direct speech.

   Henrietta exclaimed that she was eager to learn Russian.

   ....

   I asked Marcus if he wanted to join art club with me.

   ....

   (2 marks)

8. There are six punctuation mistakes in this passage.
   Rewrite the passage, correcting them all.

   > After we ate dinner I dared my brother to blow the most enormous bubble he could. He accepted sam — always accepts a dare. He managed to produce a jaw dropping bubble. However I knew it wouldnt be long before it popped.

   ....

   ....

   ....

   ....

   ....

   (3 marks)

   Score: /12

Spring Term: Workout 6

Warm up

1. Circle the verb in each sentence.

   The sensible voice in Arif's head warned him of the dangers.

   Rachael foolishly gambled all of her points on the final question.

   (1 mark)

2. In each pair, underline the sentence that uses dashes correctly.

   a) They'll arrive — in an hour.　　I can't eat that — it has gone cold.

   b) I don't know — shall we ask?　　These pastries — are from the bakery.

   (1 mark)

3. Draw lines to match each word to the correct prefix.

   | in | il | im | ir |

   proper　　reversible　　literate　　expensive

   (1 mark)

4. Read the two sentences below. Explain how the meaning of the sentence is changed when the comma is added.

   You should try cooking Graham.

   You should try cooking, Graham.

   ....

   ....

   (1 mark)

5. Complete each sentence with the plurals of the words in brackets.

   Those .... (*sheep*) saved the day and became .... (*hero*).

   Sink your .... (*tooth*) into this pie made from .... (*cactus*).

   (1 mark)

6. Complete each sentence by putting the verb into the tense or form given.

   I .... to take my dragon rollerskating. (*to want — simple past*)

   Last year, he .... to having terrible balance. (*to confess — past perfect*)

   However, he .... to join me anyway. (*to decide — present perfect*)

   I .... hopeful he won't set the rink on fire. (*to be — present*)

   (2 marks)

7. There are four spelling errors in this passage.
   Rewrite the passage correctly on the lines below.

   His conclucion that ostriches and giraffes aren't compatable is ridiculus.
   They both have elongated necks, so they view things from the same pespective.

   ....

   ....

   ....

   (2 marks)

8. There are six grammatical mistakes in this passage.
   Rewrite the passage, correcting them all.

   The lighthouse sit on a hill. Mr Acorn, which lives inside the lighthouse, telled me that there is a unbelievable view from the top. On a clear day, you can seeing for miles. However, today I can't see nothing because of all the fog.

   ....

   ....

   ....

   ....

   ....

   (3 marks)

   Score: /12

Spring Term: Workout 7

Warm up

1. Underline the preposition in each sentence.

   If you head towards the supermarket and keep walking, you'll find the library.

   Hattie was strolling along the canal when she saw the swans.

   (1 mark)

2. Circle the comma that should be removed from each sentence.

   Although, Dean was tired, he still wanted to read a chapter of his book.

   Asim enjoys windsurfing, whereas I prefer paddleboarding, and canoeing.

   (1 mark)

3. Circle the adjectives and underline the adverbs in the passage below.

   > We got up early to admire the dazzling sunrise. Bright colours bled into the clouds as the sun's rays gradually lit up the sky.

   (1 mark)

4. Add the correct word from the brackets to each sentence, then underline the relative clause.

   This is Lexi, ... short story came in first place. *(which / whose)*

   The milkman, ... usually comes at 7 am, is late. *(which / who)*

   Isla read the message inside the bottle .... she found. *(whose / that)*

   (2 marks)

5. Add the correct word from the brackets to each sentence so it uses the subjunctive.

   Kezia wishes that she .... an astronaut. *(was / were)*

   I suggest that she .... her drum a bit quieter. *(play / plays)*

   (1 mark)

6. Underline the correct spelling of the words in bold to complete the sentences below.

   The new house **feachures / features** a balcony that overlooks the pond.

   We were grateful that our hotel room in Spain had **ventilasion / ventilation**.

   Cheung tried to **reasure / reassure** his sister before her first day of school.

   Fatima did lots of **preparatian / preparation** for the cupcake-baking contest.

   (2 marks)

7. Write one sentence containing an apostrophe to show possession and one sentence containing an apostrophe used for contraction.

   possession: ....

   ....

   contraction: ....

   ....

   (2 marks)

8. There are three spelling errors in each passage. Rewrite the passages correctly on the lines below.

   "That singer is stewpendous," murmurred Asha.
   Her friend agreed that she was quiet marvellous.

   ....

   ....

   My interaction with Soren was breif. However,
   I know he is parcial to playing golf ocassionally.

   ....

   ....

   (2 marks)

   Score: ☐ /12

Spring Term: Workout 8

Warm up

1. In each pair, circle the word that is spelt correctly.

   a) desimilar   dissimilar   b) disactivate   deactivate

   c) disheard   misheard   d) unfamiliar   infamiliar

   (1 mark)

2. Write down the sentence type of each sentence below.

   Don't steal my roast potatoes!   ....

   You promised you would tell me a story.   ....

   What a fantastic day it has been!   ....

   (1 mark)

3. Add '-ant' or '-ent' to complete the words in the sentences below.

   Though he made a vali............... effort, Daryll did not run fast enough.

   I am hesit............... to let the postman come near my dog.

   He noticed a signific............... improvement in my singing ability.

   She is said to be a highly compet............... ice sculptor.

   (2 marks)

4. Underline the conjunction in each sentence. Then, write 'co-ordinating' or 'subordinating' to show what type of conjunction each one is.

   I brought a huge suitcase, yet I forgot the sun cream.   ....

   Talia wants to order a pizza whereas I'd rather cook.   ....

   Since it is dark outside, we are going to set off early.   ....

   (2 marks)

5. Add the six missing commas to the passage below.

Earlier Henry our gardener said that his lawn mower was missing. Although we searched the garden the garage and the back of his van it was nowhere to be found. Curiously the neighbours have just started mowing their lawn.

(2 marks)

6. Rewrite the second sentence, adding one hyphen so that it has the same meaning as the first sentence.

   There were men with six arms sitting on the pier.

   There were six armed men sitting on the pier.

   ....
   (1 mark)

7. There are six places where non-Standard English has been used in the passage below. Rewrite the passage so it uses only Standard English.

   Today, I been to the new trampoline park in town. We was there for hours and it was really fun. I should of worn them socks that you can hire for the session, though, cos mine didn't have no grip and I kept slipping over.

   ....
   ....
   ....
   ....
   ....
   (3 marks)

   Score: /12

Spring Term: Workout 9

> **Warm up**
>
> 1. In each pair, circle the word that is spelt correctly.
>
>   a) gallopped   galloped   b) applied   applyed
>
>   c) emerging   emergeing   d) forbiding   forbidding
>
>   *(1 mark)*
>
> 2. Tick the sentence where the main clause is underlined.
>
>   Cy made banana bread for his friends <u>as he had some ripe bananas</u>. ☐
>
>   <u>Nell caught the ball</u> that Aleeza threw across the enormous field. ☐
>
>   *(1 mark)*

3. Write 'time', 'place' or 'cause' next to each sentence to show what the underlined conjunction in each sentence is expressing.

   <u>Wherever</u> we go, we always run into Sahil. ....

   I'll have a nap <u>once</u> I've fixed the sink. ....

   Ava tried the okra <u>as</u> she'd not had it before. ....

   (1 mark)

4. Add commas to the second sentence in each pair so that it has the same meaning as the first sentence.

   Paula thought about the question with Dulcie and Sonia before they all answered.

   Before answering Paula Dulcie and Sonia thought about the question.

   Zak turned around as he slowly came to understand he was being watched.

   Zak turned around slowly realising there was someone watching him.

   (1 mark)

5. Rewrite the sentence below, correcting the spelling mistakes.

   The dekline of bird species creates a conserning legasy.

   ....

   (1 mark)

6. Add a suffix to each of the nouns below to make them into adjectives.

   body ....   collapse ....

   misery ....   heaven ....

   (2 marks)

7. Add a suitable pronoun in each of the gaps to complete the passage below.

   Sara doesn't see Parneet and Ewan very often as .... live far away.

   Whenever her friends visit, they bring .... Ewan's special boysenberry jam. Parneet grows the boysenberries and picks .... just for Ewan to make the jam. Sara loves to put .... on her toast in the mornings.

   (2 marks)

8. There are six punctuation marks missing from the passage below.
   Rewrite the passage, adding in the missing punctuation.

   > We discussed these topics at the school council meeting the possibility of a school wide treasure hunt litter on the playground, which was brought up last time; what we could do in activities week (3rd-9th June; the talent show and the school newsletter

   ....

   ....

   ....

   ....

   ....

   ....

   (3 marks)

   Score: ☐ / 12

Spring Term: Workout 10

Warm up

1. Underline the verbs in each of the sentences below.

    Keeley often gardens in the spring and she plants many beautiful flowers.

    Before the contest, Freyja practised her speech so she knew it from memory.

    (1 mark)

2. Draw lines to match each word to an appropriate prefix.

    | auto | anti | mis | dis |

    continue   mobile   freeze   handle

    (1 mark)

3. Add brackets in the correct places to the sentences below.

    Oslo the capital of Norway has many popular tourist attractions .

    Lucy bought the doorstop shaped like an ostrich from the charity shop .

    Sea stars are aquatic water-dwelling animals that are also called starfish .

    (1 mark)

4. Circle the correct word to complete each sentence below.

    At the end of the presentation, we will **summarify** / **summarise** our findings.

    Fraser used a filter to **purifise** / **purify** the water from the river.

    If plant and animal remains are left in sediment, they might **fossilise** / **fossilify** .

    (1 mark)

5. Write whether the adverb is showing that something is certain or possible on the lines.

    We will *absolutely* visit you over the summer.   ....

    Perhaps Ezra will finish mending the clock soon.   ....

    Abdur *undoubtedly* sent you a postcard from Brazil.   ....

    (1 mark)

6. Write down a homophone on the lines for each of the words below.

   dual ....   horse ....

   flee ....   mussel ....

   ring ....   baron ....

   (2 marks)

7. Rewrite the sentences below in the voice given in brackets.

   Penicillin was discovered by Alexander Fleming in 1928. *(active voice)*

   ....

   Hashir booked the castle-tour tickets in advance. *(passive voice)*

   ....

   (2 marks)

8. Rewrite the passage below, changing any reported speech to direct speech.

   > Mr Chortle, a clown, told our reporter that the theft of helium balloons has ruined his shows. The police officers in charge of the case said they would be grateful for any information. They then went on to say that they cannot comment further at this time.

   ....

   ....

   ....

   ....

   (3 marks)

   Score: ☐ / 12

Spring Term: Workout 11

Warm up

1. Circle all the words that are spelt correctly below.

   anxcious   vivacious   flirtatious

   infecsious   nutritious   subconsious

   (1 mark)

2. Underline the expanded noun phrase in each sentence below.

   Later on, Sorrel climbed the old, gnarled tree at the end of the garden.

   Ernest looked after lots of antique ceramic ornaments of great value.

   (1 mark)

3. Draw lines to show if the adverbs below express time, place or cause.

   time   place   cause

   nearby   consequently   soon   thus

   (1 mark)

4. Use an apostrophe to shorten the phrases below and write the correct shortened forms on the line.

   that is   ....   will not   ....

   might not   ....   who would   ....

   (1 mark)

5. Rewrite the sentences below using either a dash or a semicolon.

   Dylan likes the trumpet Tessa hates the noise.

   ....

   One thing was clear we were locked out of the house.

   ....

   (2 marks)

6. Underline the possessive pronoun in each sentence.

   Hers was the best out of all the model trains.

   He thought his time was more important than theirs.

   I need gloves — Carmen took mine when she forgot her mittens.

   (1 mark)

7. Add a suffix to each of the words in bold to finish the sentences below.

   Our town has many **prosper**................................ small businesses.

   They are **confer**................................ about this matter as we speak.

   Generally speaking, **venom**................................ scorpions are best avoided.

   This ticket isn't **transfer**................................, so you can't use it on this train.

   (2 marks)

8. Six of the singular words in the passage below should be plural.
   Rewrite the passage, correcting all the mistakes.

   The old television was a wreck. Its antenna were bent, and it sounded like there were fly buzzing in the two speaker. Tia could only hear faint echo of a documentary about three goose that had befriended some baby calf.

   ....

   ....

   ....

   ....

   ....

   ....

   (3 marks)

   Score: ☐ /12

Spring Term: Workout 12

Warm up

1. Circle the modal verb in each sentence below.

    Where shall we go next?   Elsbeth will repair the shelf later.

    Should you be doing that?   Matheus said he might visit São Paulo.

    (1 mark)

2. Underline the relative clause in each sentence below.

    Petra will call the lady who has the spare key.

    I made a tapestry we plan to hang on the wall.

    (1 mark)

3. Circle the correct spelling to complete each sentence.

    Their interior design choices had a **rustick** / **rustic** feel about them.

    The **president** / **presidant** of the organisation has a meeting this morning.

    Do you have a **license** / **licence** for that flying carpet?

    (1 mark)

4. Add the suffix to each word and write the new word on the line.

    examine + ation   ....

    erode + sion   ....

    install + ation   ....

    (1 mark)

5. Add commas in the correct places in the sentences below.

    Later that day we went for a walk visited a market and saw the beach.

    All of a sudden the clouds descended and we were surrounded by fog.

    With a flourish the actor bowed as flowers were thrown at the stage.

    Gordon found many insects birds fungi and plants.

    (2 marks)

6. For each sentence, write 'S' if the apostrophe is used to show singular possession, or 'P' if it is used to show plural possession.

   We will announce the results of the men's egg-and-spoon race. ....

   Mehreen sneezed as the book's pages were extremely dusty. ....

   The octopus's camouflage allows it to hide from predators. ....

   Gryff liked the tulips' petals and how bright their colours were. ....

   (1 mark)

7. Rewrite the sentences in the form given in brackets.

   Melody contemplated walking the Offa's Dyke Path. *(past perfect)*

   ....

   Barney attended chess club for many years. *(present perfect)*

   ....

   (2 marks)

8. Rewrite the passage below, correcting any spelling mistakes.

   Your excelent performances have prompted much considerasion from the judges. We listened to the experts' insightfull comments and we will consider the possibilaty of multiple winners. Please wait patiently for our desision.

   ....
   ....
   ....
   ....
   ....

   (3 marks)

   Score: /12

Summer Term: Workout 1

> **Warm up**
>
> 1. In each pair, underline the sentence where the preposition shows why something happens.
>
>   a) We will return at nightfall.   The road is closed due to a flood.
>
>   b) The runner stopped for a drink.   We have to watch the next episode.
>
>   *(1 mark)*
>
> 2. Circle the determiners in the sentences below.
>
>   Most pets are messy, but my kitten is very tidy.
>
>   Each person playing gets three marbles to start.
>
>   *(1 mark)*

3. Add dashes in the correct places to the passage below.

   I am so proud of my new clothing designs the colours of the fabrics look very vivid. Mr Crowe my textiles teacher commended me on my patterns.

   (1 mark)

4. Tick each group of words that is a clause.

   they stopped chatting ☐   after a very long walk ☐

   the large flock of birds ☐   where I travelled once ☐

   (1 mark)

5. Rewrite the sentences below so they use Standard English.

   Georgie threw the ball powerful to the batter.

   ....

   Belle ain't split the money equally between us.

   ....

   (2 marks)

6. Underline the conjunction that has been used incorrectly in each sentence.
   Then, write a conjunction on the dotted line that could replace it.

   You are welcome to call until you need to. ....

   Our feet were aching while we continued. ....

   (1 mark)

7. There are six spelling mistakes in the passage below.
   Rewrite the passage, correcting all of the mistakes.

   > I was greatly dissapointed. The fields were not green, but yellow, due to the feirce temperateures — a far cry from the pictures I'd seen in the catalogs. I tried not to critiscise everything I passed, but I couldn't hide my displeazure.

   ....

   ....

   ....

   ....

   ....

   ....

   (3 marks)

8. Add a word from the same word family as the word in brackets to complete the sentence below.

   Zainab suddenly .... she had left her backpack. (*memorise*)

   The group of .... went backstage to change costumes. (*react*)

   Leonardo lifted his dance partner into the air .... (*steadiness*)

   The man had a charming smile and .... eyes. (*capture*)

   (2 marks)

   Score: ☐ /12

Summer Term: Workout 2

Warm up

1. Underline the adverbial phrases in the sentences below.

   Beaming from ear to ear, Kieran ripped open the wrapping paper.

   I had my first clarinet recital the day before yesterday.

   (1 mark)

2. In each pair, circle the word that is spelt correctly.

   a) chemical   chemichal   b) conscience   consience

   c) literature   litrature   d) compremise   compromise

   (1 mark)

3. In each of the sentences below, circle the subject and underline the object.

   The jury are still yet to reach a verdict.

   At dinner, Yara and Missy spoke to Violet.

   (1 mark)

4. Add a comma to each sentence below to change its meaning.

   Adi likes karaoke music, chess and reading magazines.

   Dana followed the speedy cow on a rusty bike.

   I would say it's about time we hoover up Jeremiah.

   (1 mark)

5. In each sentence, underline the word that uses the incorrect prefix.
   Then, write the correct spelling of the word on the line.

   The performance was disappointing and decouraging.   ....

   They reduced 5% off the price of the imperfect goods.   ....

   The ruling is dissatisfactory and must be reconsidered.   ....

   We apologise for the misprint — it was a missight.   ....

   (2 marks)

6. Rewrite the list below using bullet points. Use punctuation after each point.

   I have conditions for a housemate they must be polite, they must be quiet, they must be tidy (especially in the kitchen) and they must like pets — I own a puppy.

   ....
   ....
   ....
   ....
   ....
   (2 marks)

7. Complete the sentences using a modal verb to make them less certain.
   Use a different modal verb for each one.

   You .... need to buy some more books.

   They .... get battered haddock from the chip shop.
   (1 mark)

8. Rewrite the passage below in the active voice.

   > Roberto was invited to the party by Louisa. A disco theme was chosen by her. Roberto was driven by a taxi to the venue, where he was greeted by his friends. The dance floor was filled by people and delicious food was served by waiters.

   ....
   ....
   ....
   ....
   ....
   (3 marks)

   Score: ☐ /12

Summer Term: Workout 3

Warm up

1. In each pair, underline the sentence that uses a preposition.

    a) The circus will soon head north.   We played a card game at home.

    b) She lives above the bookshop.   The cat meowed as birds flew above.

    (1 mark)

2. Tick the sentence that uses commas correctly.

    The fortune teller, a peculiar woman called Luna Moon, told me my fate. ☐

    Jensen, does competitive duck herding, a lesser-known hobby, on his farm. ☐

    (1 mark)

3. Add the suffix in the brackets to the word in bold.

    Naomi and I have **differ** (ing) ………………………… opinions on broccoli.

    The leaders are attending a **confer** (ence) ………………………… in Australia.

    (1 mark)

4. In each of the sentences below, underline the adverb that shows where things are.

    Please wait there and I will be with you soon.

    Eventually, I quietly moved upstairs.

    Oscar politely stepped forwards to greet him.

    (1 mark)

5. Use a prefix to give each of these words their opposite meaning.

    personal   …………………………

    sensitive   …………………………

    rational   …………………………

    (1 mark)

6. Complete the table below by writing a synonym and antonym for each word.

	Synonym	Antonym
vital		
gentle		
authentic		

(2 marks)

7. Write 'colon' or 'semicolon' next to each sentence to show which punctuation mark could replace the word in italics.

Trixie enjoys orienteering *and* Haitao likes crochet. ....

Caspar took a detour *because* the road was closed. ....

Selena gasped *as* there were paw prints on her floor. ....

The restaurant was full *whereas* the café was empty. ....

(2 marks)

8. Rewrite the passage below so it uses more formal language.

> I dropped out of badminton class because playing multiple sports a week knackered me. My trainer was a bit gutted, but I am chuffed with my decision. It was daft to start so many sports in the first place, wasn't it?

....

....

....

....

....

....

(3 marks)

Score: / 12

Summer Term: Workout 4

Warm up

1. Circle the apostrophes that are used incorrectly in the sentences below.

   Edmund doesn't think its' bad, but it isn't his favourite place to have a coffee.

   I won't be able to come to the party you're throwing — whens' the next one?

   (1 mark)

2. In each pair, underline the sentence that uses a relative pronoun.

   a) Indie shook his hand confidently.   It was the very first day that we met.

   b) He's in the room where we do art.   Yuki left it on the mantelpiece for her.

   (1 mark)

3. Choose the correct form of the verb in brackets to complete the sentences.

   We .... the flight to Brazil. (*booking / have booked / books*)

   Piper .... her music theory exam. (*pass / has passed / past*)

   (1 mark)

4. Add commas in the correct places in the passage below.

   After a while Harley Phoebe and Dan came back. Flustered they were carrying a broken umbrella a soggy map and an empty flask.

   (1 mark)

5. Some of the plurals in the passage below are wrong.
   Underline the mistakes, then write the correct plurals on the lines.

   > The children sifted through boxs of antiques. There were treasures of all kinds: pieces of jewellery, toys, watches, glasses, keys, pennys, photos of people's lifes. The children invented theorys about the stories behind the series of objects.

   ....

   ....

   (2 marks)

6. Tick each sentence where the subordinate clause is underlined.

   Yasmin loves to play chess <u>although her grandad always beats her</u>. ☐

   <u>The candle flickered</u> as the cold draught came in from outside. ☐

   After last year's success, <u>we will hold another cheese-rolling race</u>. ☐

   (1 mark)

7. Rewrite the words in italics with the correct comparatives or superlatives.

   Kay is *bad* than Chris at javelin, but she's the *good* at discus.

   ....

   Thriller is the *exciting* genre, while horror is the *frightening*.

   ....

   (2 marks)

8. Rewrite the passage below, replacing the words in bold with synonyms and the underlined words with antonyms.

   > I ambled through the <u>lifeless</u> meadow. The air was filled with the <u>revolting</u> smell of flowers and the **pleasant** sound of the birds. Suddenly, a **menacing** tractor **growled** into life, disturbing the <u>chaotic</u> serenity of my walk.

   ....

   ....

   ....

   ....

   ....

   ....

   (3 marks)

   Score: ☐ /12

Summer Term: Workout 5

> **Warm up**

1. Write down whether each sentence is a statement (S) or a command (C).

   We instructed them to take the next left. ....

   Give me a call when you get home. ....

   You probably need something to eat. ....

   (1 mark)

2. In each pair, underline the sentence where the conjunction expresses place.

   a) He has a scar where he broke his arm.   I get freckles when the sun comes out.

   b) I went to Italy as my family lives there.   Owen sees her wherever he goes.

   (1 mark)

3. Underline the adverbial phrase in each sentence.

   I hope to be a qualified astronaut in the next five years.

   With a skip in her step, Kazu went to collect her certificate.

   Josh, exhausted, fell asleep on the bus home.

   (1 mark)

4. Add two paragraph markers (//) to the passage below.

   Ryan traipsed through the forest. He was lost. "Not again," he sighed, sitting on a nearby log. It was wet and uneven. Back at camp, Rosie was wondering where Ryan was. He'd been gone for hours. Where could he be?

   (1 mark)

5. Write the correct spelling of the words in italics on the dotted lines.

   Caitlin paid the *check* into her bank account.   ....

   Amira met up with her *colleages* after work.   ....

   (1 mark)

6. Circle the incorrect semicolons in the sentence below. Rewrite the sentence, replacing the incorrect semicolons with the correct punctuation.

   For the play; we painted sets; we sewed costumes for the cast; who tried them on; and we made props.

   ....

   ....
   (2 marks)

7. Rewrite the sentences below so they use the subjunctive.

   The homeowners ask us to wipe our feet.

   ....

   My job requires me to dress smartly.

   ....
   (2 marks)

8. Rewrite the passage below, correcting the six grammatical mistakes.

   Tamsin and me usually spends the weekends baking because her dad let we use his recipe books. We have made so much different recipes, but our favourites are the sweet treats because Tamsin and I all love sugar.

   ....

   ....

   ....

   ....

   ....

   ....
   (3 marks)

   Score: ☐ /12

Summer Term: Workout 6

Warm up

1. Tick the sentence where the main clause is underlined.

   Hailey swam forty lengths of the pool <u>before she went in the jacuzzi</u>. ☐

   Due to a change of plans, <u>Nick is no longer going to the paint party</u>. ☐

   (1 mark)

2. Circle the incorrect dash in each sentence below.

   Priya gets a takeaway every Friday — she almost always — gets Chinese food.

   I went with Tyler — to his pottery class — I found it very therapeutic.

   (1 mark)

3. Draw lines to match each underlined noun to the correct box.

   Steph rose to <u>fame</u> as a TV presenter.

   We gave Grandma a <u>bunch</u> of flowers.

   I tried on some new <u>shoes</u> yesterday.

   Brian strummed a tune on his <u>guitar</u>.

   concrete noun

   abstract noun

   collective noun

   (1 mark)

4. Rewrite this sentence to make it more formal.

   He hasn't forgotten about the science project, has he?

   ....

   (1 mark)

5. Rewrite the sentences below, correcting the verbs so the tenses are consistent.

   Currently, I am singing, Jo drew and Khalid reads.

   ....

   Last year, Ria buys a dog, quit her job and moves house.

   ....

   (2 marks)

6. Write down the object of each sentence on the lines.

   Zahra bought a hot chocolate in town.   ....

   The rock band loudly performed a song.   ....

   (1 mark)

7. Complete the words in each sentence with the correct prefix.

   The lifeguards keep new swimmers under close .... vision.

   Aaron says tomorrow's forecast is for .... mittent rain.

   Aziz's nurse dabbed his graze with some .... septic.

   All the processes in this factory are fully .... mated.

   (2 marks)

8. There are six spelling mistakes in the passage below.
   Rewrite the passage, correcting the mistakes.

   > My mischievious cat, Mr Whiskers, also refered to as 'Whizz', had been coghing all week. I assumed he was sufferring from a horrendus case of the flu, so Mia, our vet, examined him. After looking thouhtful for a moment, she just got Whizz to heave up a giant hairball.

   ....

   ....

   ....

   ....

   ....

   ....

   (3 marks)

   Score: ☐ / 12

Summer Term: Workout 7

> **Warm up**
>
> 1. Underline the pronouns in the sentences below.
>
>   Aleksander baked us some scones and they were very flavoursome.
>
>   My friend Chelsea said she wants to visit Denmark because it is pretty.
>
>   *(1 mark)*
>
> 2. In each pair, circle the word that is spelt correctly.
>
>   a) televise   tellyvise   b) sickening   sickenning
>
>   c) disquallify disqualify   d) dignified   dignifyed
>
>   *(1 mark)*

3. In each sentence, circle the word with a silent letter
   and underline the word with an unstressed vowel.

   He sat in the bedroom combing his marvellous red locks.

   Bart's manager has been assigning him lots of different tasks this week.

   (1 mark)

4. For each sentence, write down a co-ordinating conjunction
   you could use to replace the underlined conjunction.

   I hoped for sun, <u>yet</u> the sky remained cloudy and grey.   ....

   We could go on the rollercoaster <u>and</u> the log flume.   ....

   (1 mark)

5. Two of the sentences below are not written in Standard English.
   Rewrite them using Standard English on the lines below.

   Our trainer thought us rowed competent.   Her match was postponed indefinitely.

   Rashida asked me to cut her hair neatly.   Them buses let us down very frequent.

   ....

   ....

   (2 marks)

6. Complete each sentence with a different adverb to show how probable it is. The words in brackets tell you whether each sentence should be certain or possible.

   Cece will .... come if she hears we are serving curry. (*certain*)

   Kian should .... set up the games console beforehand. (*possible*)

   (1 mark)

7. Write down the longest noun phrase from each sentence on the lines.

   Hakeem visited the local farmer's market and he bought lots of red, juicy tomatoes.

   ....

   Diana baked a tasty, warm carrot cake to eat with a cup of tea.

   ....

   (2 marks)

8. There are six spelling and punctuation mistakes in this passage. Rewrite the passage, correcting them all.

   > You must do these things before you lock up;
   > - Dissinfect the till and lock its draw;
   > - Take out the bin bags and the recycling seperately
   >
   > Finally, turn off the lights.

   ....

   ....

   ....

   ....

   ....

   (3 marks)

   Score: /12

Summer Term: Workout 8

> **Warm up**
>
> 1. In each sentence, circle the verb that is in the wrong tense.
>
>   Melanie gets up, showers, brushes her teeth, eats and went to school.
>
>   Paul loaded the car with fishing equipment, starts it and drove off.
>
>   *(1 mark)*
>
> 2. Underline the sentence that contains a spelling mistake.
>
>   The wildlife sanctuary looks after numerous endangered species.
>
>   The detectives reveiwed the CCTV footage for signs of the criminal.
>
>   *(1 mark)*

3. Circle the commas which are used incorrectly in the sentences below.

   The most sought-after item, at the auction, an abstract painting, sold for thousands.

   Sal's part-time job, babysitting, for his next-door neighbours, pays well.

   Cold water swimming, also, known as winter swimming, is a growing trend.

   (1 mark)

4. Write the determiner in each sentence on the lines.

   We have enough wetsuits for everyone.   ....

   Dom gave each family member gifts.   ....

   (1 mark)

5. Underline the modal verb in each sentence. Then, rewrite the sentences using a different modal verb to make them less certain. Use a different verb each time.

   Destiny must practise her solo before the show.

   ....

   Fumiko's obsession with sloths will fade.

   ....

   (2 marks)

6. Add a word from the same word family as the word in brackets to complete the sentences below.

   Ibrahim forages for mushrooms in the .... (*deforestation*)

   The .... of the world is now over 8 billion. (*popular*)

   Trains, trams and buses are types of public .... (*portable*)

   Wendy asked her coach to .... his instructions. (*clear*)

   (2 marks)

7. Complete the sentence below by adding a main clause.

   They wanted to try skydiving but ....

   ....

   (1 mark)

8. There are six spelling mistakes in the passage below. Rewrite the passage, correcting all of the mistakes.

   Pete has impossably bad luck, so he has become very supersticious. He is suspitious of black cats, he's overcausious around mirrors, and he finds Friday 13th intolereble as he seems to get a bike puncsure every time it occurs.

   ....

   ....

   ....

   ....

   ....

   ....

   (3 marks)

   Score: ☐ / 12

Summer Term: Workout 9

> **Warm up**
>
> 1. Add a prefix to give each of these words their opposite meaning.
>
>   ………foreseen   ………replaceable   ………complete
>
>   *(1 mark)*
>
> 2. Circle the correct words to complete each sentence below.
>
>   I had **a / an / the** amazing day with **a / an / the** good friend of mine.
>
>   **A / An / The** most visited attraction in Paris is **a / an / the** Eiffel Tower.
>
>   *(1 mark)*

3. Underline the relative clause in each of the sentences below.

   The diver, who was visibly shaking with nerves, approached the board.

   I drew a picture which ended up winning a prize in the art fair.

   (1 mark)

4. Read the two sentences below. Explain how the meaning of the sentence is changed when the hyphen is added.

   Where is the little used casserole dish?   Where is the little-used casserole dish?

   ……

   ……

   (1 mark)

5. Complete each sentence with a different preposition. The words in brackets tell you whether the preposition should show time, place or cause.

   The suspect must have been here ………………………… dawn. *(time)*

   ………………………… the sea, there was an abandoned lighthouse. *(place)*

   I can't sleep ………………………… the noisy elevator next to my hotel room. *(cause)*

   The hair salon is ………………………… the bakery and the bookshop. *(place)*

   (2 marks)

6. Add dashes in the correct places in the sentences below.

   I invited Kara — the new student at school — to sit with me.
   Luis always beats me at tennis — his serve is very powerful.
   (1 mark)

7. Rewrite the passage below as a single sentence using semicolons.

   This is how to set up your computer:
   - Unbox your monitor, unwrap it and place it on your desk.
   - Plug in the red wire (not the brown one).
   - Press the oval-shaped start button.

   ....

   ....

   ....

   ....
   (2 marks)

8. Rewrite the passage below, replacing the words in bold with synonyms and the underlined words with antonyms.

   > I felt rather **grumpy** when I woke up as my dad's <u>thoughtful</u> decision to mow the lawn — an apparently **crucial** task at 7 am — had **disrupted** my lie-in. I drank some <u>bland</u> orange juice and hoped the day would soon <u>deteriorate</u>.

   ....

   ....

   ....

   ....

   ....
   (3 marks)

   Score: ☐ /12

Summer Term: Workout 10

Warm up

1. In each pair, underline the sentence that contains a preposition phrase.

    a) Theo sighed, for he was lost.   They got to the theatre by bus.

    b) Let's go bowling on Friday.   I enjoy reading and playing chess.

    (1 mark)

2. Circle the correct punctuation mark to go in the gap in each sentence.

    "I think it's time we all went on holiday ...." said Julie.   **, OR .**

    Felipe inquired, "What on earth are you doing here ...."   **! OR ?**

    "What a breathtaking and impressive parade that was ...."   **. OR !**

    (1 mark)

3. In each group of words, circle the word that is not part of the same word family as the other words.

    a) discontent   contend   contented   contentment

    b) significantly   signifies   signature   insignificant

    (1 mark)

4. Complete the sentences using a modal verb to make them more certain. Use a different modal verb for each one.

    You .... wear a disguise or else they will recognise you.

    Damian and Kate .... arrive together at around 9 pm.

    (1 mark)

5. Use a subordinating conjunction to add a subordinate clause to the sentences below. Use a different conjunction for each one.

    Jane wants to visit Egypt ....

    Dhriti got a new hat ....

    (1 mark)

6. There are six spelling mistakes in the passage below. Cross out the incorrect words, then write the correct spellings above the mistakes.

The careers presentacian was intriging, and the photographer's talk was fasinating. He displayed lots of landscapes on the projector screen, and shared informasion about his photography techniks that we found espetially interesting.

(2 marks)

7. Rewrite the sentences below so that they are in the passive voice.

Thousands of people attended the concert.

....

Mara and Declan both tidied the house.

....

(2 marks)

8. There are six punctuation and grammar mistakes in the passage below. Rewrite the passage, correcting all of the mistakes.

> Although Me and Maeve were desperate to go on them scooters over there we didn't have permission. It was Gio our (camp leader) what saved the day. As long as we wore helmets he allowed us to ride them.

....

....

....

....

....

(3 marks)

Score: /12

Summer Term: Workout 11

Warm up

1. Underline the word that has a silent letter in each sentence.

   Riley found it amusing that Custard was so fascinated by his reflection.

   The politician ran a convincing campaign and was finally elected.

   (1 mark)

2. Circle the modal verb in each sentence.

   What do you think we should do about the flea infestation?

   Carly might buy a new pair of ballet slippers to replace her old ones.

   (1 mark)

3. In each pair, tick the sentence that uses Standard English.

   a) We was running in the park. ☐   Don't you have any notepads? ☐

   b) Imran doesn't like folk music. ☐   They seen that sci-fi film before. ☐

   c) I could of been famous. ☐   You don't have any red bicycles. ☐

   (1 mark)

4. Add the missing punctuation to the sentence below.

   Don't you think woodlice look like small armadillos Rob pondered

   (1 mark)

5. Add a prefix to the words in brackets to complete the sentences below.

   We will be .... multiple candidates for this job. (*viewing*)

   I thought the film's ending was a frustrating .... (*climax*)

   The singer began writing her .... at age fifteen. (*biography*)

   Jamal wore a cape to emulate his favourite .... (*hero*)

   (2 marks)

6. Unscramble the words in italics to complete the sentences below.

   I felt *reveilde* .... when I found out I had passed the exam.

   They used trickery to *zisee* .... and imprison the evil ruler.

   Yasmin showers daily to maintain good personal *geinyhe* ....

   (1 mark)

7. Rewrite the sentences below so that they are in the past progressive form.

   We climbed to the top of the hill at sunrise.

   ....

   Elena laughed at the witty comedy routine.

   ....

   (2 marks)

8. There are six spelling and punctuation mistakes in the passage below. Rewrite the passage, correcting all of the mistakes.

   > Teddys long, complex excercise routine begins with him lifting waits until his arms get tired. When he's regained his staminar it's time for some lunges a few squats and a couple of sit-ups.

   ....

   ....

   ....

   ....

   ....

   (3 marks)

   Score: /12

Summer Term: Workout 12

Warm up

1. In each pair, circle the word that is spelt correctly.

    a) misread   missread   b) iresistible   irresistible

    c) disuade   dissuade   d) imeasurable   immeasurable

    (1 mark)

2. In each group of words, underline the word that is an adjective.

    a) health   expect   musically   uninterested

    b) plead   effort   vast   underneath

    (1 mark)

3. Complete the sentences using a conjunction which shows when things happen. Use a different conjunction in each sentence.

    I emptied the box .... I assembled the desk.

    The opera went on .... the middle of the night.

    (1 mark)

4. In each of the sentences below, underline the relative pronoun and circle the possessive pronoun.

    I watched a double bassist whose performance inspired me to play mine.

    The treasure, which Benjamin had spent years looking for, was finally his.

    (1 mark)

5. Tick each sentence that uses dashes correctly.

    My kittens — Pip and Pop — both prefer eating mackerel to tuna. ☐

    Someone has stolen my favourite bookmark and — I am furious. ☐

    Last week — I saw a pair of trousers I liked — so I bought them. ☐

    We were suddenly plunged into darkness — there was a powercut. ☐

    (1 mark)

6. Complete the table below by correctly adding each suffix to the root words.

Root word	-ed	-ing
exile		
regret		
supply		

(2 marks)

7. Rewrite the sentences below, adding an adverbial phrase to each one.

We sprinted to catch the train.

....

Liza goes for long hikes.

....

(2 marks)

8. There are six punctuation and grammar mistakes in the passage below. Rewrite the passage, correcting them all.

> "This is the terriblest day ever." Cory groaned, his face becoming sweaty. His car, who was brand new had been stuck in some mud for fortyfive minutes, and his attempts to push it out had made things worst.

....

....

....

....

....

(3 marks)

Score: / 12

Answers

Autumn Term

Workout 1 — pages 2-3

1. **a)** potatoes, oranges
    b) kangaroos, parties
    (1 mark for all 4 correct)

2. very, lazily, suddenly
    (1 mark for all 3 correct)

3. "Hey!" I shouted. "Can you help me with these heavy bags?"
    (1 mark for all correct)

4. E.g. thought, doughnuts, through
    (1 mark for all 3 correct)

5. who, whom, Who
    (1 mark for all 3 correct)

6. Sunil forgot one thing: the gym wasn't open.
    My dad wanted a pet bird; I wanted a snake.
    (2 marks available — 1 mark for each correct sentence)

7. wholly, cruise, waste, coarse
    (2 marks available — 1 mark for every 2 correct words)

8. E.g. Lulu glided adeptly across the water. Her hands clutched the metal bar. It became instantly clear to any spectators that this was not her first time on the wakeboard. She was, in fact, an expert.
    (3 marks available — 1 mark for each sensible division of the text)

Workout 2 — pages 4-5

1. substan — tial   benefi — cial
    antiso — cial   impar — tial
    (1 mark for all 4 correct)

2. **a)** That's Mrs Roberts's house.
    b) The orchestra's rehearsal isn't going well.
    (1 mark for both correct)

3. Riva wants me to go to the concert with her, but I'm quite tired.
    He likes dressing up as a pirate because it makes him look tougher.
    We can go to the park down the road if it stops raining soon.
    (1 mark for all 3 correct)

4. Since I left my umbrella at home, I should probably borrow yours.
    E.g. You need a comma when the subordinate clause appears at the beginning of the sentence.
    (2 marks available — 1 mark for the comma correctly added, 1 mark for a correct explanation)

5. delay — abstract
    pride — collective
    shelf — concrete
    (1 mark for all 3 correct)

6. successful, argument, responsible, brightness
    (2 marks available — 1 mark for every 2 correct words)

7. Hae bought delicious cakes from her favourite family-owned bakery.
    (1 mark)

8. You are craving a bowl of my world-famous soup. We are beginning with a chopped onion, then tomatoes, garlic and stock. You are tasting the soup occasionally while it is cooking. When the mixture is bubbling, I am squeezing in the secret ingredient — ketchup.
    (3 marks available — 1 mark for every 2 verbs correctly rewritten)

Workout 3 — pages 6-7

1. **a)** confidence   **b)** distance
    c) importance   **d)** audience
    (1 mark for all 4 correct)

2. **a)** In the distance, I saw a huge tree.
    b) Sadly, he stole my bow tie last week.
    (1 mark for both correct)

3. fictitious, malicious, corruption
    (1 mark for all 3 correct)

4. dash, brackets, brackets
    (1 mark for all 3 correct)

5. Our team's flag was captured. Instructions have been provided.
    (1 mark for both correct)

6. possibly, likely
    E.g. It's definitely not the best weather for an ice cream, but I'll certainly have one.
    (2 marks available — 1 mark for underlining the adverbs, 1 mark for rewriting the sentence with 2 different sensible adverbs)

7. faster, biggest
    more, noisiest
    (2 marks available — 1 mark for every 2 correct comparatives or superlatives)

8. At eight last night, my next-door neighbour pranked me by hiding my favourite gnome. I couldn't believe her cheek. When I retrieved him, she shrieked with laughter and denied being the gnome thief.
    (3 marks available — 1 mark for every 2 words correctly rewritten)

Workout 4 — pages 8-9

1. **a)** There's no chance we're losing.
    b) He doesn't have time for a nap.
    (1 mark for both correct)

2. moisture, exposure, creature
    (1 mark for all 3 correct)

3. C, P, C
    (1 mark for all 3 correct)

4. We had two options: hide behind a tree or run away from the bear.
    (1 mark for adding a suitable clause)

5. E.g. I would like that maroon jumper although it's expensive.
    Kyla likes to go fishing whereas I find it a bit dull.
    (2 marks available — 1 mark for each suitable conjunction)

6. My mum's shopping list included these items:
    • pineapple juice,
    • one pint of skimmed milk,
    • six sausages,
    • a bag of self-raising flour (the supermarket brand).
    (2 marks available — 1 mark for every 2 correct bullet points. Either commas or semicolons can be used)

Answers

Answers

7. during, until, after, before
   (1 mark for all 4 correct)

8. My friend <u>has</u> bought a lie detector machine and we <u>are</u> going to take turns doing a test. It'll be fun but I <u>am</u> a bit nervous. He is going to ask me questions and if the machine <u>beeps</u>, it means my answers <u>are</u> lies. I <u>hope</u> I pass the test!
   (3 marks available — 1 mark for every 2 verbs correctly rewritten)

Workout 5 — pages 10-11

1. a) My sleeveless shirt is in the wash.
   b) I've lost my left glove.
   (1 mark for both correct)

2. Claudia couldn't stand the taste of citrus fruits.
   The council has recently decided to expand the school.
   (1 mark for both correct)

3. freezes, caught
   (1 mark for both correct)

4. Unless the weather improves<u>,</u> the match will be called off.
   E.g. You need a comma when the subordinate clause appears at the beginning of the sentence.
   (2 marks available — 1 mark for the comma correctly added, 1 mark for a correct explanation)

5. A solitary boat floated on <u>the unusually calm, crystal water</u>.
   <u>The horse's long, flowing mane</u> was plaited for the showjumping contest.
   <u>The ominous, grey thunder clouds</u> covered the once-peaceful valley.
   (1 mark for all 3 correct)

6. my drums, Fahad and I, her bike, Polly
   (2 marks available — 1 mark for every 2 correct nouns)

7. The bird flew <u>gracefully</u> over the field, preparing to snatch its <u>prey</u> with claws as sharp as <u>knives</u>.
   (1 mark for all 3 correct)

8. E.g. Rudy <u>hurled</u> open the curtains and <u>beamed</u>. Fresh, <u>glistening</u> snow blanketed everything. He was <u>elated</u> — school would be cancelled, so he would <u>avoid</u> an entire day of lessons. He called his neighbour, Amelie, and <u>enquired</u> if she wanted to go sledging.
   (3 marks available — 1 mark for every 2 suitable synonyms)

Workout 6 — pages 12-13

1. Dani gave surfing <u>a</u> try but she was scared of <u>the</u> waves.
   Alexis had <u>an</u> excellent run and was <u>the</u> fastest skier.
   (1 mark for all 4 correct)

2. He wanted to visit her <u>but</u> she lived too far away.
   <u>If</u> I had wings, I would fly to Spain.
   (1 mark for both correct)

3. a) trough, cough
   b) brought, sought
   (1 mark for both correct)

4. When the project is complete, | we will throw an enormous party.
   They are the people | who decided to live in the depths of the forest.
   We are staying in the entrance of the building | until Harry arrives.
   The winning team beamed with pride | when the final whistle blew.
   (2 marks available — 1 mark for every 2 lines in the correct place)

5. The tower is <u>notable</u> for its <u>considerable</u> height. The top floor is only <u>accessible</u> via a steep stairway.
   (1 mark for all 3 correct)

6. international, anticlockwise, interactive, supersized, anticlimactic, autograph
   (3 marks available — 1 mark for every 2 words correct)

7. The dish needs these things<u>:</u> mushrooms, peppers and onions.
   Pablo has four dogs<u>;</u> Jamie has a rabbit and three cats.
   (2 marks available — 1 mark for each sentence correctly rewritten)

8. E.g.

Formal style	Informal style
Give me the key immediately.	Gimme the key pronto.
I shall endeavour to attend.	I'll try to come.
I expect it is fantastic.	I bet it's brill.

(1 mark for 3 suitable sentences)

Workout 7 — pages 14-15

1. Which of those plates of food is mine? — question
   Katy swore she would never eat spinach again. — statement
   How amazing that performance was! — exclamation
   Come into the kitchen immediately! — command
   (1 mark for all 4 correct)

2. a) The picnic was prepared by Granny.
   b) Faisal was embraced by Immy.
   (1 mark for both correct)

3. My favourite music genres are pop, country and reggae.
   (1 mark)

4. Valeria <u>would</u> have gone to the party but she was already busy.
   Tomek is going to arrive at 7 so I <u>must</u> prepare dinner before then.
   Asa has been saving his pocket money so he <u>can</u> buy a saxophone.
   (1 mark for all 3 correct)

5. E.g. disastrous, flawless, religious, speechless
   (2 marks available — 1 mark for every 2 adjectives correct)

6. Samara bought herself a new bike and <u>she</u> rode <u>it</u> home.
   My friends enjoy eating pizza so <u>they</u> eat <u>it</u> every Friday.
   (2 marks available — 1 mark for each sentence correct)

7. as I was scrapbooking
   he makes his own cheese
   (1 mark for both correct)

Answers

8. The boat swayed fiercely from side to side. Suddenly, there was an almighty crash and Callie plunged into the dark water. She began to swim. // After what seemed like a lifetime, she made it to the shore and collapsed in a heap, panting heavily. // "Hello! Is anyone here?" she shouted. "Where am I?" //
In the nearby village, Nauris had decided to stroll to the beach. He was enjoying the fresh air when he heard what sounded like someone shouting for help. He hurried towards the sound.
Any suitable reasons for starting the new paragraphs, e.g.
Because time moved on.
Because someone started to speak.
Because the place changed.
(3 marks available — 1 mark for each paragraph marker correctly added with a suitable reason given)

Workout 8 — pages 16-17

1. a) They always like baking.
   b) He usually eats out on Fridays.
   (1 mark for both correct)

2. Yesterday, Ben played golf, I went shopping and Rex sleeps.
   She believes that sandwiches were the best food and eats them daily.
   (1 mark for both correct)

3. Olga loves to dance: she dances for three hours a week.
   Felix's goldfish has an unusual name: it is called Pumpkin.
   (1 mark for both correct)

4.
Concrete noun	Collective noun	Abstract noun
bottle	flock	loyalty
taxi	fleet	trust

(2 marks available — 1 mark for every 3 correct)

5. Omid cooked a roast dinner for his brother and sister in law.
   Mina recounted the money to check that she had enough.
   Hallie set a short term goal of exercising every day for a week.
   (1 mark for all 3 correct)

6. identified, identifying
   rebelled, rebelling
   (1 mark for all 4 correct)

7. Claude Monet (a famous artist) painted water lilies.
   We couldn't believe our eyes — the dolphin was waving at us.
   Shrove Tuesday (known as Pancake Day) is the day before Lent begins.
   Matilda laughed sheepishly — nobody else was in fancy dress.
   (2 marks available — 1 mark for every 2 sentences punctuated correctly)

8. Winning seemed inconceivable. The referee's unjust decision to disallow a goal jeopardised the Pudgley Pioneers' chances. But after the coach's electrifying pep talk, they equalised. Then, in highly irregular circumstances, the keeper's goal kick found their opponents' net, securing the Pioneers' victory.
   (3 marks available — 1 mark for every 2 words correctly rewritten)

Workout 9 — pages 18-19

1. adjectives — friendly, homely
   adverbs — quickly, suddenly
   (1 mark for all 4 correct)

2. The actor delivered her monologue.
   The scenery is extremely picturesque.
   (1 mark for both correct)

3. My robot is asking if the humans can give him a hug.
   I had an interest in the most popular poet of the century.
   (1 mark for all 4 correct)

4. the sun, I, This drawer
   (1 mark for all 3 correct)

5. I was reluctant to enter the unexplored cave.
   The scientists conducted an experiment in the lab.
   (1 mark for both correct)

6. On the top floor of the manor, there was a dimly lit attic.
   E.g. You need a comma after a fronted adverbial.
   (2 marks available — 1 mark for the comma correctly added, 1 mark for a correct explanation)

7. He's a new addition to our league.
   Accept this gift as a token of my gratitude.
   (2 marks available — 1 mark for each sentence correct)

8. Though they all warned me against living in an igloo, my friends' remarks didn't deter me. So here's what I did: I packed a bag, travelled across the globe (on several planes) and arrived in Greenland's capital, Nuuk, all alone.
   (3 marks available — 1 mark for every 2 mistakes corrected)

Workout 10 — pages 20-21

1. While I jogged, my hair swished in the breeze.
   She implied that the chorus of the song is boring.
   (1 mark for all 4 correct)

2. Callum hadn't seen his dog in hours.
   There wasn't any milk in the fridge.
   (1 mark for both correct)

3. derail, disinfect, mishear, disadvantage
   (1 mark for all 4 correct)

4. My pet hamster is definitely greedier than yours.
   I lent her mine because her tambourine had broken.
   Jacob might want a treehouse if we show him ours.
   (1 mark for all 3 correct)

5. E.g. I decided to take the bus yesterday evening.
   (1 mark for a suitable adverbial phrase)

Answers

6.

Root word	-ed	-ing
empty	emptied	emptying
achieve	achieved	achieving
patrol	patrolled	patrolling

(2 marks available — 1 mark for every 3 correctly spelt words)

7. Could you please tell me the time asked Aliz.
"Could you please tell me the time?" asked Aliz.
(2 marks available — 1 mark for ticking the correct sentence, 1 mark for the correctly rewritten sentence)

8. Tomorrow, I am <u>going</u> to a water park, and I <u>am</u> planning to spend all day in the water. I <u>can't</u> wait: last time I went I <u>flew</u> down the slides and <u>floated</u> along the lazy river. I just <u>hope</u> it doesn't rain tomorrow!
(3 marks available — 1 mark for every 2 verbs correctly rewritten)

Workout 11 — pages 22-23

1. a) Wednesday b) comp<u>a</u>ny
   c) voluntary d) anim<u>a</u>l
   (1 mark for all 4 correct)

2. <u>In case it was dark outside</u>, Alexa brought a torch.
   We'll have to hurry up <u>in order to reach the top in time for sunset</u>.
   (1 mark for both correct)

3. They moved me from the beginner class to the <u>intermediate</u> class.
   The <u>automotive</u> museum is where they keep all the old cars.
   Clean your hands with <u>antibacterial</u> soap for thirty seconds.
   (1 mark for all 3 correct)

4. That possum is prone to biting, however friendly he <u>may</u> seem.
   <u>Shall</u> we have a slice of chocolate cake with our cup of tea?
   (1 mark for both correct)

5. Kellie climbed straight over the fence; Tina tried to open the lock.
   The songbirds chirped; the dragonflies flitted through the rushes.
   (1 mark for both correct)

6. This mouldy cheese is <u>well</u> <u>gross</u>.
   — e.g. very, disgusting
   That <u>bloke</u> just told a <u>rubbish</u> story!
   — e.g. man, dreadful
   (2 marks available — 1 mark for underlining all 4 informal words, 1 mark for all 4 suitable formal replacements)

7. I am taking my cousin to the dentist. We are driving for six hours to get to the beach.
   (2 marks available — 1 mark for each sentence correctly rewritten)

8. On our <u>adventurous</u> trip to the <u>famous</u> Great Barrier Reef, we learnt that <u>corrosion</u> is a threat to the area. The damage humans have done may not be <u>reversible</u> — we must take <u>caution</u> and try to be more <u>sustainable</u> in future.
   (3 marks available — 1 mark for every 2 words correctly rewritten)

Workout 12 — pages 24-25

1. I <u>exercise</u> by going to a <u>dance</u> class <u>once</u> a week and riding my bike.
   (1 mark for all 3 correct)

2. Once he has eaten his lunch, Adam will go for a walk.
   Even though we lost the match, our spirits remained high.
   (1 mark for both correct)

3. time — after, before
   place — everywhere
   cause — so
   (1 mark for all 4 correct)

4. Unfortunately, I think <u>your new cat-themed calendar</u> is missing a page.
   There is a fluffy sheep jumping on <u>a huge, blue and red bouncy castle</u>.
   I think <u>the mysterious hole at the end of the garden</u> leads to a secret cave.
   (1 mark for all 3 correct)

5. steady + ly, mature + ity
   (1 mark for both correct)

6. E.g. We got a new lamp in place of the old one.
   E.g. We put the lamp back on the shelf.
   (2 marks available — 1 mark for each suitable explanation)

7. potentially — U
   inevitably — C
   definitely — C
   perhaps — U
   (2 marks available — 1 mark for underlining all 4 adverbs, 1 mark for correctly identifying what all 4 adverbs show)

8. The air <u>was becoming</u> colder. I <u>was approaching</u> the door steadily. Sweat <u>was beginning</u> to form on my brow and goosebumps <u>were popping</u> up on my arms. The floorboards <u>were groaning</u> at full volume. Under pressure, I <u>was starting</u> to panic.
   (3 marks available — 1 mark for every 2 verbs correctly rewritten)

Spring Term

Workout 1 — pages 26-27

1. a) backlog b) physique
   c) anorak d) dialogue
   (1 mark for all 4 correct)

2. The dog jumped <u>off</u> the sofa and ran <u>under</u> the table.
   <u>Within</u> days, the caterpillar had turned <u>into</u> a butterfly.
   (1 mark for all 4 correct)

3. had learnt / learned, have eaten
   (1 mark for both correct)

4. Lucas<u>,</u> known to his friends as Luke<u>,</u> loves films. Paige<u>,</u> Luke's sister<u>,</u> works for a film studio. Last Friday<u>,</u> Paige's boss gave her some tickets to a premiere. Being a kind sister<u>,</u> Paige decided to take Luke to the premiere with her.
   (2 marks available — 1 mark for every 3 commas added correctly)

Answers

5. E.g. They <u>must</u> have taken a shortcut to get home before us.
    Jordan's train <u>will</u> have arrived at the station by now.
    We <u>might</u> have gone to the wrong café by accident.
    (1 mark for 3 suitable modal verbs)

6. those, many, our
    (1 mark for all 3 correct)

7. E.g. I spoke to Jess, the lawyer — she lives next door<u>;</u> Masood, Barry's friend<u>;</u> and Kev, the security guard<u>.</u>
    (2 marks available — 1 mark for writing a single sentence, 1 mark for all 3 punctuation marks)

8. Minnie had to be <u>subtle</u> to avoid her enemies. She had <u>disguised</u> herself in <u>armour</u> and now approached the <u>castle</u>. Huge dogs guarded the gates, <u>gnawing</u> on bones. Minnie clenched her fists so tightly her <u>knuckles</u> turned white.
    (3 marks available — 1 mark for every 2 words correctly rewritten)

Workout 2 — pages 28-29

1. a) endeavour   b) arrest
    (1 mark for both correct)

2. Tori told Danielle she fancied a walk, so the two of them went out.
    (1 mark)

3. inferring, offered, referral
    (1 mark for all 3 correct)

4. Fenhua passed the old bench <u>where he used to sit</u>. — relative clause
    <u>Milo is going to the gig instead</u> as Faye can't go. — main clause
    Djamila, <u>who I sit with in history</u>, is a hockey player. — relative clause
    <u>I went to a music festival</u> which lasted all week. — main clause
    (1 mark for all 4 correct)

5. E.g. The group is going to the skate park <u>nearby</u>.
    I am meeting my stepbrother <u>tomorrow</u> for an ice lolly.
    (1 mark for 2 suitable adverbs)

6. "Is that what I think it is<u>?</u>" whispered Imamu.
    Ayaan screamed, "What an utterly horrifying creature<u>!</u>"
    <u>"</u>Let's get out of here before it wakes up<u>,</u>" uttered Paisley.
    (2 marks available — 1 mark for every 3 correct punctuation marks)

7. a) Joel and me get on really good.
       — Joel and <u>I</u> get on really <u>well</u>.
    b) I think them dance so elegant.
       — I think <u>they</u> dance so <u>elegantly</u>.
    (2 marks available — 1 mark for each sentence correctly underlined and rewritten)

8. Writing a book takes patience and <u>resilience</u>, so <u>ultimately</u> you should choose a subject that's of <u>significance</u> to you. <u>Frankly</u>, if you're hesitant about the topic, you'll be <u>likely</u> to abandon your book in an <u>instant</u>.
    (3 marks available — 1 mark for every 2 words correctly rewritten)

Workout 3 — pages 30-31

1. a) unthinkable   b) unknowingly
    c) uninspiring   d) undecided
    (1 mark for all 4 correct)

2. The student's new books<u>'</u> were going to be used in Mr Fosters<u>'</u> class. Chanels<u>'</u> favourite sport is rugby; she play<u>'</u>s for her school's team.
    (1 mark for all 4 correct)

3. I would ban loud chewing if I were Prime Minister.
    It is absolutely essential that Omari get plenty of rest.
    (1 mark for both correct)

4. The bowling alley is closed <u>—</u> let's come back tomorrow.
    I haven't skied in years <u>—</u> last time I broke my ankle.
    Ron is out <u>—</u> he is having lunch at a café in town.
    (1 mark for all 3 correct)

5. E.g. Cami learnt to speak some Japanese <u>before</u> she moved to Tokyo.
    I no longer eat dairy products <u>as</u> I am now a vegan.
    Patrick won't read a book <u>unless</u> it is in the fantasy genre.
    (1 mark for 3 suitable subordinating conjunctions)

6.
Adjective	Comparative	Superlative
bad	worse	**worst**
expensive	**more expensive**	**most expensive**
silly	**sillier**	silliest

    (2 marks available — 1 mark for every 3 correct words)

7. This autumn, we move to Newcastle and buy a house.
    I spoke to Benedika and we chose to leave the band.
    (2 marks available — 1 mark for each sentence correctly rewritten)

8. I was <u>conscious</u> that I wanted to be more <u>social</u> in my community, so I took up a new hobby: <u>martial</u> arts. In my <u>initial</u> lessons, I was pretty <u>atrocious</u>. I was trying far too many <u>overambitious</u> moves for a beginner.
    (3 marks available — 1 mark for every 2 words correctly rewritten)

Workout 4 — pages 32-33

1. a) stabilise   b) personify
    c) truly   d) drastically
    (1 mark for all 4 correct)

2. It's supposed to rain | so we have got an umbrella.
    Holly wants to be a landscaper | and she is very talented.
    Josiah wants to attend university | before he goes travelling.
    (1 mark for all 3 correct)

3. Afterwards, I will go to training.
    Did Aia pass on Sam's message?
    (1 mark for both correct)

Answers

4. Here's the agenda: paint the kitchen ceiling where the roof leaked; tear off the wallpaper under the stairs; and replace the showerhead in the bathroom.
   (1 mark for all 3 correct)

5. The <u>manufactured</u> <u>furniture</u> was <u>remeasured</u> to ensure it was correct.
   (1 mark for all 3 words correctly rewritten)

6. Joe shone the torch over the dirt-covered plaque. // "Vinegrove Mansion," he said, reading the sign aloud. // Later that night, the house was all he could think about. He pondered why so grand an estate had been left abandoned.
   Any suitable reasons for starting the new paragraphs, e.g.
   Because someone started to speak.
   Because time moved on.
   (2 marks available — 1 mark for each paragraph marker correctly added with a suitable reason given)

7. E.g. Kito is going rollerblading with Mercy on <u>Friday</u>.
   The <u>range</u> of mountains was majestic.
   Flo accepted her award with <u>gratitude</u>.
   Caden grabbed his <u>coat</u> and ran out the door.
   (2 marks available — 1 mark for every 2 suitable nouns)

8. Council members <u>have</u> approved plans to build a housing estate on our park. My son <u>feels</u> so upset — the children <u>use</u> this space every day. My neighbours and I <u>are</u> furious, so we <u>are</u> planning to object when the members next <u>meet</u>.
   (3 marks available — 1 mark for every 2 verbs correctly rewritten)

Workout 5 — pages 34-35

1. **b)** D & F
   (1 mark)

2. **a)** The house with the blue door is theirs.
   b) My bag is similar to hers.
   (1 mark for both correct)

3. I designed some s<u>c</u>enery for the play's autumnal setting.
   Gloria thinks the dress is w<u>h</u>ite, but I'd say it's closer to a sa<u>l</u>mon pink.
   (1 mark for both correct)

4. Eitan thought he <u>must</u> have imagined the flying raccoon.
   <u>Will</u> you carry the shopping bags for the rest of the journey?
   If you want some company, I <u>could</u> join you on your trip.
   (1 mark for all 3 correct)

5. aught — ought
   distrought — distraught
   ruff — rough
   breakthrew — breakthrough
   (2 marks available — 1 mark for every 2 correctly underlined and rewritten words)

6. This is Casey's telephone number, <u>isn't it?</u>
   <u>Aren't</u> you supposed to be at hockey practice?
   Let me know if you <u>wanna</u> come swimming with us.
   (1 mark for all 3 correct)

7. E.g. Henrietta exclaimed, "I am eager to learn Russian!"
   E.g. I asked Marcus, "Do you want to join art club with me?"
   (2 marks available — 1 mark for each sentence correctly rewritten)

8. After we ate dinner, I dared my brother to blow the most enormous bubble he could. He accepted — Sam always accepts a dare. He managed to produce a jaw-dropping bubble. However, I knew it wouldn't be long before it popped.
   (3 marks available — 1 mark for every 2 mistakes corrected)

Workout 6 — pages 36-37

1. The sensible voice in Arif's head <u>warned</u> him of the dangers.
   Rachael foolishly <u>gambled</u> all of her points on the final question.
   (1 mark for both correct)

2. **a)** I can't eat that — it has gone cold.
   b) I don't know — shall we ask?
   (1 mark for both correct)

3. in — expensive   il — literate
   im — proper   ir — reversible
   (1 mark for all 4 correct)

4. The comma shows that Graham is being told to try cooking rather than being cooked.
   (1 mark)

5. Those <u>sheep</u> saved the day and became <u>heroes</u>.
   Sink your <u>teeth</u> into this pie made from <u>cacti</u>.
   (1 mark for all 4 correct)

6. I <u>wanted</u> to take my dragon rollerskating.
   Last year, he <u>had confessed</u> to having terrible balance.
   However, he <u>has decided</u> to join me anyway.
   I <u>am</u> hopeful he won't set the rink on fire.
   (2 marks available — 1 mark for every 2 correct verbs)

7. His <u>conclusion</u> that ostriches and giraffes aren't <u>compatible</u> is <u>ridiculous</u>. They both have elongated necks, so they view things from the same <u>perspective</u>.
   (2 marks available — 1 mark for every 2 words correctly rewritten)

8. The lighthouse <u>sits</u> on a hill. Mr Acorn, <u>who</u> lives inside the lighthouse, <u>told</u> me that there is <u>an</u> unbelievable view from the top. On a clear day, you can <u>see</u> for miles. However, today I can't see <u>anything</u> because of all the fog.
   (3 marks available — 1 mark for every 2 mistakes corrected)

Workout 7 — pages 38-39

1. If you head <u>towards</u> the supermarket and keep walking, you'll find the library.
   Hattie was strolling <u>along</u> the canal when she saw the swans.
   (1 mark for both correct)

Answers

2. Although(,) Dean was tired, he still wanted to read a chapter of his book.
   Asim enjoys windsurfing whereas I prefer paddleboarding(,) and canoeing.
   (1 mark for both correct)

3. You should have circled: dazzling, Bright
   You should have underlined: early, gradually
   (1 mark for all 4 correct)

4. This is Lexi, **whose** short story came in first place.
   The milkman, **who** usually comes at 7 am, is late.
   Isla read the message inside the bottle **that** she found.
   (2 marks available — 1 mark for adding the correct word to all three sentences, 1 mark for correctly underlining the relative clauses)

5. Kezia wishes that she <u>were</u> an astronaut.
   I suggest that she <u>play</u> her drum a bit quieter.
   (1 mark for both correct)

6. features, ventilation, reassure, preparation
   (2 marks available — 1 mark for every 2 correct)

7. E.g. Possession — Taylor's shoes are too small for her feet.
   Contraction — It's freezing outside today.
   (2 marks available — 1 mark for each suitable sentence)

8. "That singer is <u>stupendous</u>," <u>murmured</u> Asha. Her friend agreed that she was <u>quite</u> marvellous. My interaction with Soren was <u>brief</u>. However, I know he is <u>partial</u> to playing golf <u>occasionally</u>.
   (2 marks available — 1 mark for each passage correctly rewritten)

Workout 8 — pages 40-41

1. **a)** dissimilar **b)** deactivate
   c) misheard **d)** unfamiliar
   (1 mark for all 4 correct)

2. Don't steal my roast potatoes! — command
   You promised you would tell me a story. — statement
   What a fantastic day it has been! — exclamation
   (1 mark for all 3 correct)

3. Though he made a vali<u>ant</u> effort, Daryll did not run fast enough.
   I am hesit<u>ant</u> to let the postman come near my dog.
   He noticed a signific<u>ant</u> improvement in my singing ability.
   She is said to be a highly compet<u>ent</u> ice sculptor.
   (2 marks available — 1 mark for every 2 correct)

4. I brought a huge suitcase, <u>yet</u> I forgot the sun cream. — co-ordinating
   Talia wants to order a pizza <u>whereas</u> I'd rather cook. — subordinating
   <u>Since</u> it is dark outside, we are going to set off early. — subordinating
   (2 marks available — 1 mark for underlining all the conjunctions, 1 mark for correctly writing the type of conjunction for all sentences)

5. Earlier, Henry, our gardener, said that his lawn mower was missing. Although we searched the garden, the garage and the back of his van, it was nowhere to be found. Curiously, the neighbours have just started mowing their lawn.
   (2 marks available — 1 mark for every 3 commas correctly added)

6. There were six-armed men sitting on the pier.
   (1 mark)

7. E.g. Today, I <u>went</u> to the new trampoline park in town. We <u>were</u> there for hours and it was really fun. I should <u>have</u> worn <u>those</u> socks that you can hire for the session, though, <u>because</u> mine didn't have <u>any</u> grip and I kept slipping over.
   (3 marks available — 1 mark for every 2 examples of non-Standard English rewritten)

Workout 9 — pages 42-43

1. **a)** galloped **b)** applied
   c) emerging **d)** forbidding
   (1 mark for all 4 correct)

2. Nell caught the ball that Aleeza threw across the enormous field.
   (1 mark)

3. place, time, cause
   (1 mark for all 3 correct)

4. Before answering, Paula, Dulcie and Sonia thought about the question.
   Zak turned around, slowly realising there was someone watching him.
   (1 mark for all 3 correct)

5. The <u>decline</u> of bird species creates a <u>concerning</u> <u>legacy</u>.
   (1 mark for all 3 correct)

6. bodily, collapsible, miserable, heavenly
   (2 marks available — 1 mark for every 2 words correct)

7. Sara doesn't see Parneet and Ewan very often as <u>they</u> live far away. Whenever her friends visit, they bring <u>her</u> Ewan's special boysenberry jam. Parneet grows the boysenberries and picks <u>them</u> just for Ewan to make the jam. Sara loves to put <u>it</u> on her toast in the mornings.
   (2 marks available — 1 mark for every 2 pronouns correct)

8. We discussed these topics at the school council meeting: the possibility of a school-wide treasure hunt; litter on the playground, which was brought up last time; what we could do in activities week (3rd-9th June); the talent show; and the school newsletter.
   (3 marks available — 1 mark for every 2 punctuation marks correctly added)

Answers

Workout 10 — pages 44-45

1. Keeley often <u>gardens</u> in the spring and she <u>plants</u> many beautiful flowers.
   Before the contest, Frejya <u>practised</u> her speech so she <u>knew</u> it from memory.
   (1 mark for all 4 correct)

2. auto — mobile   anti — freeze
   mis — handle   dis — continue
   (1 mark for all 4 correct)

3. Oslo (the capital of Norway) has many popular tourist attractions.
   Lucy bought the doorstop (shaped like an ostrich) from the charity shop.
   Sea stars are aquatic (water-dwelling) animals that are also called starfish.
   (1 mark for all 3 pairs correct)

4. At the end of the presentation, we will <u>summarise</u> our findings.
   Fraser used a filter to <u>purify</u> the water from the river.
   If plant and animal remains are left in sediment, they might <u>fossilise</u>.
   (1 mark for all 3 correct)

5. certain, possible, certain
   (1 mark for all 3 correct)

6. duel, hoarse, flea, muscle, wring, barren
   (2 marks available — 1 mark for every 3 words correct)

7. Alexander Fleming discovered penicillin in 1928.
   The castle-tour tickets were booked in advance by Hashir.
   (2 marks available — 1 mark for each sentence correct)

8. E.g. "The theft of helium balloons has ruined my shows," Mr Chortle, a clown, told our reporter.
   "We would be grateful for any information," said the police officers in charge of the case. They then went on to say, "We cannot comment further at this time."
   (3 marks available — 1 mark for each example of direct speech correctly punctuated)

Workout 11 — pages 46-47

1. vivacious, flirtatious, nutritious
   (1 mark for all 3 correct)

2. Later on, Sorrel climbed <u>the old, gnarled tree at the end of the garden</u>.
   Ernest looked after <u>lots of antique ceramic ornaments of great value</u>.
   (1 mark for both correct)

3. time — soon
   place — nearby
   cause — consequently, thus
   (1 mark for all 4 correct)

4. that's, won't, mightn't, who'd
   (1 mark for all 4 correct)

5. Dylan likes the trumpet; Tessa hates the noise.
   One thing was clear — we were locked out of the house.
   (2 marks available — 1 mark for each correct punctuation mark)

6. <u>Hers</u> was the best out of all the model trains.
   He thought his time was more important than <u>theirs</u>.
   I need gloves — Carmen took <u>mine</u> when she forgot her mittens.
   (1 mark for all 3 correct)

7. Our town has many prosper<u>ous</u> small businesses.
   They are confer<u>ring</u> about this matter as we speak.
   Generally speaking, venom<u>ous</u> scorpions are best avoided.
   This ticket isn't transfer<u>able</u>, so you can't use it on this train.
   (2 marks available — 1 mark for every 2 suffixes correctly added)

8. The old television was a wreck. Its <u>antennae</u> were bent, and it sounded like there were <u>flies</u> buzzing in the two <u>speakers</u>. Tia could only hear faint <u>echoes</u> of a documentary about three <u>geese</u> that had befriended some baby <u>calves</u>.
   (3 marks available — 1 mark for every 2 words correctly rewritten)

Workout 12 — pages 48-49

1. Where <u>shall</u> we go next?
   Elsbeth <u>will</u> repair the shelf later.
   <u>Should</u> you be doing that?
   Matheus said he <u>might</u> visit São Paulo.
   (1 mark for all 4 correct)

2. Petra will call the lady <u>who has the spare key</u>.
   I made a tapestry <u>we plan to hang on the wall</u>.
   (1 mark for both correct)

3. Their interior design choices had a <u>rustic</u> feel about them.
   The <u>president</u> of the organisation has a meeting this morning.
   Do you have a <u>licence</u> for that flying carpet?
   (1 mark for all 3 correct)

4. examination, erosion, installation
   (1 mark for all 3 correct)

5. Later that day, we went for a walk, visited a market and saw the beach.
   All of a sudden, the clouds descended and we were surrounded by fog.
   With a flourish, the actor bowed as flowers were thrown at the stage.
   Gordon found many insects, birds, fungi and plants.
   (2 marks available — 1 mark for every 3 commas placed correctly)

6. P, S, S, P
   (1 mark for all 4 correct)

7. Melody <u>had contemplated</u> walking the Offa's Dyke Path.
   Barney <u>has attended</u> chess club for many years.
   (2 marks available — 1 mark for each sentence correct)

8. Your <u>excellent</u> <u>performances</u> have prompted much <u>consideration</u> from the judges. We listened to the experts' <u>insightful</u> comments and we will consider the <u>possibility</u> of multiple winners. Please wait patiently for our <u>decision</u>.
   (3 marks available — 1 mark for every 2 words correctly rewritten)

Answers

Summer Term

Workout 1 — pages 50-51

1. **a)** The road is closed due to a flood.
   b) The runner stopped for a drink.
   (1 mark for both correct)

2. <u>Most</u> pets are messy, but <u>my</u> kitten is very tidy.
   <u>Each</u> person playing gets <u>three</u> marbles to start.
   (1 mark for all 4 correct)

3. I am so proud of my new clothing designs — the colours of the fabrics look very vivid. Mr Crowe — my textiles teacher — commended me on my patterns.
   (1 mark for all 3 correct)

4. they stopped chatting
   where I travelled once
   (1 mark for both correct)

5. Georgie threw the ball <u>powerfully</u> to the batter.
   E.g. Belle <u>hasn't</u> split the money equally between us.
   (2 marks available — 1 mark for each sentence correctly rewritten)

6. You are welcome to call <u>until</u> you need to. — e.g. whenever
   Our feet were aching <u>while</u> we continued — e.g. yet
   (1 mark for both words correctly underlined and replaced)

7. I was greatly <u>disappointed</u>. The fields were not green, but yellow, due to the <u>fierce</u> <u>temperatures</u> — a far cry from the pictures I'd seen in the <u>catalogues</u>. I tried not to <u>criticise</u> everything I passed, but I couldn't hide my <u>displeasure</u>.
   (3 marks available — 1 mark for every 2 words correctly rewritten)

8. Zainab suddenly <u>remembered</u> she had left her backpack.
   The group of <u>actors</u> went backstage to change costumes.
   Leonardo lifted his dance partner into the air <u>steadily</u>.
   The man had a charming smile and <u>captivating</u> eyes.
   (2 marks available — 1 mark for every 2 correct)

Workout 2 — pages 52-53

1. <u>Beaming from ear to ear</u>, Keiran ripped open the wrapping paper.
   I had my first clarinet recital <u>the day before yesterday</u>.
   (1 mark for both correct)

2. **a)** chemical **b)** conscience
   c) literature **d)** compromise
   (1 mark for all 4 correct)

3. You should have circled:
   The jury, Yara and Missy
   You should have underlined:
   a verdict, Violet
   (1 mark for all 4 correct)

4. Adi likes karaoke<u>,</u> music, chess and reading magazines.
   Dana followed the speedy cow<u>,</u> on a rusty bike.
   I would say it's about time we hoover up<u>,</u> Jeremiah.
   (1 mark for all 3 correct)

5. The performance was disappointing and <u>decouraging</u>. — discouraging
   They <u>reducted</u> 5% off the price of the imperfect goods. — deducted
   The ruling is <u>dissatisfactory</u> and must be reconsidered. — unsatisfactory
   We apologise for the misprint — it was a <u>missight</u>. — oversight
   (2 marks available — 1 mark for every 2 words correctly underlined and rewritten)

6. E.g. I have conditions for a housemate<u>:</u>
   • they must be polite<u>,</u>
   • they must be quiet<u>,</u>
   • they must be tidy (especially in the kitchen)<u>,</u>
   • they must like pets — I own a puppy.
   (2 marks available — 1 mark for every 3 punctuation marks correct. Either commas or semicolons can be used)

7. E.g. You <u>might</u> need to buy some more books.
   They <u>may</u> get battered haddock from the chip shop.
   (1 mark for 2 suitable modal verbs)

8. E.g. Louisa invited Roberto to the party. She chose a disco theme. A taxi drove Roberto to the venue, where his friends greeted him. People filled the dance floor and waiters served delicious food.
   (3 marks available — 1 mark for every 2 verbs correctly rewritten in the active voice)

Workout 3 — pages 54-55

1. **a)** We played a card game at home.
   b) She lives above the bookshop.
   (1 mark for both correct)

2. The fortune teller, a peculiar woman called Luna Moon, told me my fate.
   (1 mark)

3. Naomi and I have <u>differing</u> opinions on broccoli.
   The leaders are attending a <u>conference</u> in Australia.
   (1 mark for both correct)

4. Please wait <u>there</u> and I will be with you soon.
   Eventually, I quietly moved <u>upstairs</u>.
   Oscar politely stepped <u>forwards</u> to greet him.
   (1 mark for all 3 correct)

5. impersonal, insensitive, irrational
   (1 mark for all 3 correct)

6. E.g.

	Synonym	Antonym
vital	crucial	unnecessary
gentle	tender	rough
authentic	genuine	fake

   (2 marks available — 1 mark for every 3 sensible words)

7. semicolon, colon, colon, semicolon
   (2 marks available — 1 mark for every 2 correct)

8. E.g. I <u>quit</u> badminton class because playing multiple sports a week <u>exhausted</u> me. My trainer was a bit <u>upset</u>, but I am <u>delighted</u> with my decision. <u>Wasn't it silly</u> to start so many sports in the first place?
   (3 marks available — 1 mark for every 2 sensible replacements)

Answers

Workout 4 — pages 56-57

1. Edmund doesn't think its(') bad, but it isn't his favourite place to have a coffee.
   I won't be able to come to the party you're throwing — whens(') the next one?
   (1 mark for both correct)

2. **a)** It was the very first day that we met.
   b) He's in the room where we do art.
   (1 mark for both correct)

3. We <u>have booked</u> the flight to Brazil.
   Piper <u>has passed</u> her music theory exam.
   (1 mark for both correct)

4. After a while‸ Harley‸ Phoebe and Dan came back. Flustered‸ they were carrying a broken umbrella‸ a soggy map and an empty flask.
   (1 mark for all 4 correct)

5. boxs — boxes
   pennys — pennies
   lifes — lives
   theorys — theories
   (2 marks available — 1 mark for every 2 mistakes underlined and correctly rewritten)

6. Yasmin loves to play chess <u>although her grandad always beats her</u>.
   (1 mark)

7. worse, best
   most exciting, most frightening
   (2 marks available — 1 mark for every 2 correct comparatives or superlatives)

8. E.g. I ambled through the <u>vibrant</u> meadow. The air was filled with the <u>inviting</u> smell of flowers and the <u>delightful</u> sound of the birds. Suddenly, an <u>intimidating</u> tractor <u>snarled</u> into life, disturbing the <u>tranquil</u> serenity of my walk.
   (3 marks available — 1 mark for every 2 suitable synonyms or antonyms)

Workout 5 — pages 58-59

1. S, C, S
   (1 mark for all 3 correct)

2. **a)** He has a scar where he broke his arm.
   b) Owen sees her wherever he goes.
   (1 mark for both correct)

3. I hope to be a qualified astronaut <u>in the next five years</u>.
   <u>With a skip in her step</u>, Kazu went to collect her certificate.
   Josh, exhausted, fell asleep <u>on the bus home</u>.
   (1 mark for all 3 correct)

4. Ryan traipsed through the forest. He was lost. // "Not again," he sighed, sitting on a nearby log. It was wet and uneven. // Back at camp, Rosie was wondering where Ryan was. He'd been gone for hours. Where could he be?
   (1 mark for both correct)

5. cheque, colleagues
   (1 mark for both correct)

6. For the play(;) we painted sets; we sewed costumes for the cast(;) who tried them on; and we made props.
   For the play‸ we painted sets; we sewed costumes for the cast‸ who tried them on; and we made props.
   (2 marks available — 1 mark for both incorrect semicolons correctly circled, 1 mark for both semicolons corrected)

7. E.g. The homeowners ask that we wipe our feet.
   My job requires that I dress smartly.
   (2 marks available — 1 mark for each sentence correctly rewritten)

8. Tamsin and <u>I</u> usually <u>spend</u> the weekends baking because her dad <u>lets us</u> use his recipe books. We have made so <u>many</u> different recipes, but our favourites are the sweet treats because Tamsin and I <u>both</u> love sugar.
   (3 marks available — 1 mark for every 2 mistakes corrected)

Workout 6 — pages 60-61

1. Due to a change of plans, Nick is no longer going to the paint party.
   (1 mark)

2. Priya gets a takeaway every Friday — she almost always (—) gets Chinese food.
   I went with Tyler (—) to his pottery class — I found it very therapeutic.
   (1 mark for both correct)

3. concrete noun — shoes, guitar
   abstract noun — fame
   collective noun — bunch
   (1 mark for all 4 correct)

4. E.g. Has he forgotten about the science project?
   (1 mark)

5. Currently, I am singing, Jo is drawing and Khalid is reading.
   Last year, Ria bought a dog, quit her job and moved house.
   (2 marks available — 1 mark for each sentence correctly rewritten)

6. a hot chocolate, a song
   (1 mark for both correct)

7. The lifeguards keep new swimmers under close <u>supervision</u>.
   Aaron says tomorrow's forecast is for <u>intermittent</u> rain.
   Aziz's nurse dabbed his graze with some <u>antiseptic</u>.
   All the processes in this factory are fully <u>automated</u>.
   (2 marks available — 1 mark for every 2 correct)

8. My <u>mischievous</u> cat, Mr Whiskers, also <u>referred</u> to as 'Whizz', had been <u>coughing</u> all week. I assumed he was <u>suffering</u> from a <u>horrendous</u> case of the flu, so Mia, our vet, examined him. After looking <u>thoughtful</u> for a moment, she just got Whizz to heave up a giant hairball.
   (3 marks available — 1 mark for every 2 words correctly rewritten)

Answers

Workout 7 — pages 62-63

1. Aleksander baked <u>us</u> some scones and <u>they</u> were very flavoursome. My friend Chelsea said <u>she</u> wants to visit Denmark because <u>it</u> is pretty.
   (1 mark for all 4 correct)

2. a) televise b) sickening
   c) disqualify d) dignified
   (1 mark for all 4 correct)

3. You should have circled: combing, assigning
   You should have underlined: marvellous, different
   (1 mark for all 4 correct)

4. E.g. but, or
   (1 mark for 2 suitable conjunctions)

5. E.g. Our trainer thought we rowed competently.
   Those buses let us down very frequently.
   (1 mark for each sentence correctly rewritten in Standard English)

6. E.g. Cece will <u>definitely</u> come if she hears we are serving curry.
   Kian should <u>perhaps</u> set up the games console beforehand.
   (1 mark for 2 suitable adverbs)

7. lots of red, juicy tomatoes
   a tasty, warm carrot cake
   (1 mark for each noun phrase correctly written)

8. You must do these things before you lock up<u>:</u>
   • <u>Disinfect</u> the till and lock its <u>drawer</u>.
   • Take out the bin bags and the recycling <u>separately</u><u>;</u>
   • Finally, turn off the lights.
   (3 marks available — 1 mark for every 2 mistakes corrected)

Workout 8 — pages 64-65

1. Melanie gets up, showers, brushes her teeth, eats and <u>went</u> to school.
   Paul loaded the car with fishing equipment, <u>starts</u> it and drove off.
   (1 mark for both correct)

2. The detectives reveiwed the CCTV footage for signs of the criminal.
   (1 mark)

3. The most sought-after item(,) at the auction, an abstract painting, sold for thousands.
   Sal's part-time job, babysitting(,) for his next door neighbours, pays well.
   Cold water swimming, also(,) known as winter swimming, is a growing trend.
   (1 mark for all 3 correct)

4. enough, each
   (1 mark for both correct)

5. E.g. Destiny <u>must</u> practise her solo before the show. — Destiny might practise her solo before the show.
   Fumiko's obsession with sloths <u>will</u> fade. — Fumiko's obsession with sloths could fade.
   (2 marks available — 1 mark for each sentence correctly rewritten using a less certain modal verb)

6. Ibrahim forages for mushrooms in the <u>forest</u>.
   The <u>population</u> of the world is now over 8 billion.
   Trains, trams and buses are types of public <u>transport / transportation</u>.
   Wendy asked her coach to <u>clarify</u> his instructions.
   (2 marks available — 1 mark for every 2 correct)

7. E.g. They wanted to try skydiving but <u>they had to wait until they were 16</u>.
   (1 mark for a suitable main clause)

8. Pete has <u>impossibly</u> bad luck, so he has become very <u>superstitious</u>. He is <u>suspicious</u> of black cats, he's <u>overcautious</u> around mirrors, and he finds Friday 13th <u>intolerable</u> as he seems to get a bike <u>puncture</u> every time it occurs.
   (3 marks available — 1 mark for every 2 words correctly rewritten)

Workout 9 — pages 66-67

1. <u>un</u>foreseen, <u>ir</u>replaceable, <u>in</u>complete
   (1 mark for all 3 correct)

2. I had <u>an</u> amazing day with <u>a</u> good friend of mine.
   <u>The</u> most visited attraction in Paris is <u>the</u> Eiffel Tower.
   (1 mark for all 4 correct)

3. The diver, <u>who was visibly shaking with nerves</u>, approached the board.
   I drew a picture <u>which ended up winning a prize in the art fair</u>.
   (1 mark for both correct)

4. Without the hyphen, it means the casserole dish is both little and has been used. With the hyphen, it means the dish is not used very often.
   (1 mark)

5. E.g. The suspect must have been here <u>before</u> dawn.
   <u>By</u> the sea, there was an abandoned lighthouse.
   I can't sleep <u>due to</u> the noisy elevator next to my hotel room.
   The hair salon is <u>between</u> the bakery and the bookshop.
   (2 marks available — 1 mark for every 2 correct)

6. I invited Kara <u>—</u> the new student at school <u>—</u> to sit with me.
   Luis always beats me at tennis <u>—</u> his serve is very powerful.
   (1 mark for both correct)

7. E.g. To set up your computer<u>,</u> unbox your monitor, unwrap it and place it on your desk<u>;</u> plug in the red wire (not the brown one)<u>;</u> and press the oval-shaped start button<u>.</u>
   (2 marks available — 1 mark for writing a single sentence, 1 mark for all 4 punctuation marks)

8. E.g. I felt rather <u>irritable</u> when I woke up as my dad's <u>inconsiderate</u> decision to mow the lawn — an apparently <u>essential</u> task at 7 am — had <u>disturbed</u> my lie-in. I drank some <u>tasty</u> orange juice and hoped the day would soon <u>improve</u>.
   (3 marks available — 1 mark for every 2 sensible replacements)

Answers

Workout 10 — pages 68-69

1. a) They got to the theatre by bus.
   b) Let's go bowling on Friday.
   (1 mark for both correct)

2. "I think it's time we all went on holiday," said Julie.
   Felipe inquired, "What on earth are you doing here?"
   "What a breathtaking and impressive parade that was!"
   (1 mark for all 3 correct)

3. a) contend   b) signature
   (1 mark for both correct)

4. E.g. You must wear a disguise or else they will recognise you.
   Damian and Kate should arrive together at around 9 pm.
   (1 mark for 2 suitable modal verbs)

5. E.g. Jane wants to visit Egypt so that she can see the pyramids.
   Dhriti got a new hat because she lost her old one.
   (1 mark for 2 suitable subordinate clauses)

6. The careers presentation was intriguing, and the photographer's talk was fascinating. He displayed lots of landscapes on the projector screen, and shared information about his photography techniques that we found especially interesting.
   (2 marks available — 1 mark for every 3 words correctly rewritten)

7. The concert was attended by thousands of people.
   The house was tidied by both Mara and Declan.
   (2 marks available — 1 mark for each sentence correctly rewritten in the passive voice)

8. E.g. Although Maeve and I were desperate to go on those scooters over there, we didn't have permission. It was Gio (our camp leader) who saved the day. As long as we wore helmets, he allowed us to ride them. *(3 marks available — 1 mark for every 2 mistakes corrected)*

Workout 11 — pages 70-71

1. Riley found it amusing that Custard was so fascinated by his reflection. The politician ran a convincing campaign and was finally elected.
   (1 mark for both correct)

2. What do you think we should do about the flea infestation?
   Carly might buy a new pair of ballet slippers to replace her old ones.
   (1 mark for both correct)

3. a) Don't you have any notepads?
   b) Imran doesn't like folk music.
   c) You don't have any red bicycles.
   (1 mark for all 3 correct)

4. "Don't you think woodlice look like small armadillos?" Rob pondered.
   (1 mark for all 4 punctuation marks correctly added)

5. We will be interviewing multiple candidates for this job.
   I thought the film's ending was a frustrating anticlimax.
   The singer began writing her autobiography at age fifteen.
   Jamal wore a cape to emulate his favourite superhero.
   (2 marks available — 1 mark for every 2 correct)

6. I felt relieved when I found out I had passed the exam.
   They used trickery to seize and imprison the evil ruler.
   Yasmin showers daily to maintain good personal hygiene.
   (1 mark for all 3 correct)

7. We were climbing to the top of the hill at sunrise.
   Elena was laughing at the witty comedy routine.
   (2 marks available — 1 mark for each sentence correctly rewritten)

8. Teddy's long, complex exercise routine begins with him lifting weights until his arms get tired. When he's regained his stamina, it's time for some lunges, a few squats and a couple of sit-ups.
   (3 marks available — 1 mark for every 2 mistakes corrected)

Workout 12 — pages 72-73

1. a) misread   b) irresistible
   c) dissuade   d) immeasurable
   (1 mark for all 4 correct)

2. a) uninterested   b) vast
   (1 mark for both correct)

3. E.g. I emptied the box before I assembled the desk.
   The opera went on until the middle of the night.
   (1 mark for 2 suitable conjunctions)

4. You should have underlined: whose, which
   You should have circled: mine, his
   (1 mark for all 4 correct)

5. My kittens — Pip and Pop — both prefer eating mackerel to tuna.
   We were suddenly plunged into darkness — there was a powercut.
   (1 mark for both correct)

6.

Root word	-ed	-ing
exile	exiled	exiling
regret	regretted	regretting
supply	supplied	supplying

(2 marks available — 1 mark for every 3 correct)

7. E.g. We sprinted extremely quickly to catch the train.
   Liza goes for long hikes in the evenings.
   (2 marks available — 1 mark for each suitable adverbial phrase)

8. "This is the most terrible day ever," Cory groaned, his face becoming sweaty. His car, which was brand new, had been stuck in some mud for forty-five minutes, and his attempts to push it out had made things worse.
   (3 marks available — 1 mark for every 2 mistakes corrected)

Score Sheet

Fill in the score sheet after you finish each workout.

Write your scores below to show how you've done.
Each workout is out of 12 marks.

	Autumn Term	Spring Term	Summer Term
Workout 1			
Workout 2			
Workout 3			
Workout 4			
Workout 5			
Workout 6			
Workout 7			
Workout 8			
Workout 9			
Workout 10			
Workout 11			
Workout 12			